W9-AHH-347

Margaret Bourke-White

MARGARET BOURKE-WHITE
CLEVELAND

GREAT LIFE STORIES

Margaret Bourke-White

ADVENTUROUS PHOTOGRAPHER

CHRISTOPHER C. L. ANDERSON

FRANKLIN WATTS
A Division of Scholastic Inc.
New York Toronto London Auckland Sydney
Mexico City New Delhi Hong Kong
Danbury, Connecticut

To my grandmothers Elaine Anderson, Beatrice Gates, Irene Reid, and Ivy Smith

ACKNOWLEDGMENTS

Many thanks to Carolyn Davis, Reader Services Librarian, and her colleagues at the Special Collections Research Center of Syracuse University Library; my editor, Wendy Mead; my stepmother and special adviser, Caroline Gates Anderson; photo researcher Sarah Parrish; Makenzie Brookes; and Agha Jun.

Library of Congress Cataloging-in-Publication Data

Anderson, Christopher C. L.
Margaret Bourke-White : adventurous photographer / by Christopher C. L. Anderson.
p. cm. — (Great life stories)
Includes bibliographical references and index.
ISBN 0-531-12405-3
1. Bourke-White, Margaret, 1904–1971—Juvenile literature. 2. Women photographers—United States—Biography—Juvenile literature. 3. News photographers—United States—Biography—Juvenile literature. I. Title. II. Series.

TR140.B6A83 2005
770'.92—dc22

2004026380

Printed in the United States of America.
1 2 3 4 5 6 7 8 9 10 R 14 13 12 11 10 09 08 07 06 05

Contents

ONE An Iron Foundation 7

TWO Smokestacks on the Horizon 17

THREE The Fire Alight 29

FOUR Machine–Age Adventures 39

FIVE Behind the Machine 47

SIX Standing Her Ground 61

SEVEN Braving the Dangers 71

EIGHT Reasons to Fight 81

NINE The Price of Division 93

TEN A Will of Steel 105

Timeline 115

To Find Out More 119

A Note on Sources 121

Index 123

With her camera, Margaret Bourke-White helped the world see itself.

ONE

An Iron Foundation

Being a great photographer takes great courage and great sacrifice. No one knew this better than Margaret Bourke-White, one of the most famous photographers of the twentieth century. Bourke-White was not just a photographer, however. She was a photojournalist—someone who captured important moments on film and in words.

When Bourke-White started her career in the late 1920s, it was unusual for women to support themselves without any financial help from a husband. While the majority of women worked in the home raising families and doing housework, many were also employed as teachers and nurses, or as laborers in factories or on farms. Very few made their living from photography or reporting. Bourke-White was an innovator in this regard.

Bourke-White was not afraid to make a living by herself, nor was she afraid of the physical dangers her work involved. When covering news stories, she had to lean out of airplanes, dodge bullets, and brave extreme temperatures in order to capture unforgettable photographs. Her risk-taking energized her photographs and enthralled millions of Americans who saw her work in *Fortune* and *Life* magazines.

In Bourke-White's writing we can see how she strove to understand and explain the world. She provided insight into the reasons for the suffering of the downtrodden, speaking up for those whose stories were not being told. She interviewed men and women who were trying to improve peoples' lives and was not afraid to ask them tough questions. Her devotion to finding the truth earned her the friendship of Mohandas Gandhi, one of the greatest political and spiritual leaders of all time.

Bourke-White's promise was evident in her childhood. Her parents did not know that she would become a world-famous photojournalist, but they raised her in a way that prepared her for the challenging role she undertook.

DISCOVERING NATURE

Margaret was born in the Bronx, the northernmost part of New York City, on June 14, 1904. Her parents, Joseph and Minnie White, were thrilled that Margaret had arrived on their wedding anniversary. The family soon moved to the quiet town of Bound Brook, New Jersey, to be closer to Joe's work, developing innovations for the printing press. It is not surprising that the family left the bustling metropolis of New York City. As Joe wrote in the journal he kept when he first arrived in the city in the fall of 1888, "The trouble is in this city not the greatness of the noise, but the steadiness of it. You can't go anywhere without being in it."

In Bound Brook the family could explore forests and streams. Margaret, her older sister Ruth, and her younger brother Roger would go on nature walks with their father. Joe taught the children how to get snakes and birds to relax and rest in their hands. He taught them the names of the stars. He trained them to observe how a chrysalis opens to reveal a butterfly.

When she was a child, Margaret thought she would become a herpetologist, or an expert on reptiles and amphibians. As she recalls in her autobiography, "I pictured myself as a scientist (or sometimes as the helpful wife of a scientist), going to the jungle, bringing back specimens for natural history museums and 'doing all the things that women never do,' I used to say to myself."

Minnie, too, was fascinated by the wonders of the natural world and would

An adventurer from an early age, Margaret started out by climbing on chairs and later moved on to walking on top of fences with her sister Ruth.

share her books on wasps and grasshoppers with her children. She also focused her curiosity on her children, devotedly listening to them and recording their thoughts. On the back of a cobalt blue square of paper, Minnie wrote about Ruth: "She has been trying for some time to have me clearly understand the particular shade of blue she likes best. This is it." When her children came down with bad cases of scarlet fever, she recorded daily updates on their condition in a journal. Margaret's case of scarlet fever had her acting strangely, continuously moving and talking of the things she would like to eat. "Ordinarily, Margaret thinks little of food, and eats about enough to keep a bird alive," Minnie wrote.

The next day Margaret was still raving about food, and her desire became contagious. Minnie noted, "I had to reprove her for it, because

Outbreaks and Epidemics

The beginning of the 1900s saw many outbreaks of scarlet fever across the United States. Caused by the same bacteria that causes strep throat, the main symptoms of scarlet fever are a fever, sore throat, and a rash that can sometime spread all over the body. Left untreated, it can develop into rheumatic fever, which weakens the heart.

The influenza epidemic of 1918 killed more than half a million Americans and more than thirty million people worldwide. Unlike the most common strains of present-day flu that many people contract and recover from quickly, the influenza virus of 1918 was so powerful that a person could catch it in the daytime and be dead by evening. It caused people to bleed from their ears and nostrils. This blood would collect in their lungs, which would fill up until they died from lack of oxygen.

when Roger awakened, and heard her, he began to ask for things to eat which he would not look at when they were made ready and brought to him. So now all food conversation is 'taboo.'"

SHARED PASSIONS

As an inventor, Margaret's father Joseph needed a lot of space and quiet in order to develop his new ideas. He could often be found sitting in silence, concentrating intensely on his projects. His children learned from his behavior how important it was not to let anything interrupt one's focus. From Joseph's efforts came devices that improved the printing of newspapers, posters, and books, as well as the first Braille printing

Minnie White, Margaret's mother, was a serious woman who believed in lifelong learning. She pushed her children to overcome their fears, to always tell the truth, and to try their hardest at all they did.

Joseph White, Margaret's father, was an inventor whose hobby was photography. Margaret loved to assist him in setting up and developing his photographs.

A World in Conflict

World War I began with the murder of one person and ended with the death of millions. On June 28, 1914, a Bosnian nationalist, Gavrilo Princip, shot and killed the Austro-Hungarian Archduke Franz Ferdinand in Sarajevo. This action brought to a boil simmering conflicts between European empires, countries, and regions over land, natural resources, and models of government.

The war brought incredible suffering to the peoples of the earth. It was the first war to make widespread use of machine guns, aerial bombardment, and poison gas. In some battles, tens of thousands of lives were lost in a single day. Soldiers and civilians died not only from violence but also from starvation and disease. By the spring of 1915, the Allied powers of France, Russia, the United Kingdom, and Belgium were fighting against the Central powers of Germany, Austria-Hungary, Bulgaria, and the Ottoman Empire. Smaller countries in Europe, as well as countries on other continents, were drawn into the war. Fighting raged in Africa, the South Pacific, Russia, and Western Europe.

For almost three years the United States avoided joining in the war. Public feeling was largely against involvement. However, on April 6, 1917, the United States entered World War I on the side of the Allied powers. This was partly because of German aggression, and partly to protect business ties with England. A week later President Woodrow Wilson created the Committee on Public Information (CPI), which used the media to raise public support for the war. Posters, advertisements, rallies, and even movies and cartoons convinced many Americans that it was their patriotic duty to hate Germans and German culture. The modern advertising industry, with its sophisticated techniques of appealing to the emotions of consumers in order to sell products, has its roots in the work of the CPI.

Heavy fighting lasted through October of 1918, with the largest battles being fought in France. By the first week of November of 1918, all of the Central powers had surrendered except Germany. Then, on November 11, 1918, Germany signed an agreement to end the war. Its economy was in shambles and its monarchy overthrown. With the defeat of the Central powers and the weakening of the European Allied powers due to the costs of the war, the United States' power on the world stage grew enormously.

press. During World War I, which raged from 1914 until 1918, Margaret's father designed portable printing presses that could print maps on the battlefield. These maps, based on aerial photographs of the position of the enemy's army, would help an army plan and avoid attacks.

While his family respected his hard work and his creativity, the demands Joseph put on himself often distanced him from them. During his business trips, Minnie had to take care of three children by herself, and even when he was home he could be so lost in thought that he would not hear his family members when they were speaking to him.

On the other hand, Joseph had a sense of adventure that captivated his children. They enjoyed traveling with him to Washington, D.C., and to Canada and seeing the wonders of technology up close. When Margaret was eight, he took her to a foundry that manufactured printing presses. In the foundry, iron was heated to the point at which it became an extremely hot, bright, orange and red liquid that could be poured into a mold. Margaret thought it was the most beautiful thing she had ever seen, and it left a lasting impression on her.

DISAPPOINTMENT AND PROMISE

Margaret learned so much at home and in nature that school must have seemed dull in comparison. In high school, she was not in the popular crowd. Her clothes were not stylish enough, and her personality was too serious. She was active in school clubs and known for being smart, but this did not seem to make the boys interested in her.

At the end of her sophomore year, just before the commencement dance, she won a literary prize for one of her stories. Margaret had been taking dancing lessons and dreaming of dancing with a boy. Here was her chance. Someone would surely want to dance with the charming prizewinner. She waited all evening, but not a single boy approached her. She ended up dancing with a girl who was friends with her sister Ruth.

When Margaret was fifteen, she went to a phrenologist. Phrenologists practiced something akin to palm reading. They felt the bumps on people's heads in order to determine what their mental abilities, personality, and health concerns were. Of all the observations and suggestions Margaret's phrenologist made, two were particularly interesting. One was right on the mark, the other a little less so.

"You are always ready to go to any place that is suggested to gather news and information," she noted, "and you do not mind the trouble that you have to take in gaining that information if it is what you want." She went on to say, "You should always take photographs of places you visit, so as to give lectures afterward. This will be an outlet to your mind

Women Win the Right to Vote

In August of 1920, the Constitution of the United States was amended for the nineteenth time since its original ratification in 1788. With the addition of the Nineteenth Amendment, women were given the right to vote. Since the middle of the 1800s, women had been putting pressure on the government to grant them the right that only men enjoyed. Their movement was called the woman's suffrage movement, and Elizabeth Cady Stanton and Susan B. Anthony were two of its best-known leaders.

and will serve as a means for entertaining your friends in an agreeable manner." As an adult Margaret would indeed travel without hesitation or fear in order to capture the news. But her pictures would do much more than entertain friends. They would instruct and inspire people the world over.

In her senior year of high school, Margaret was an editor of the school yearbook and co-composed the class poem. She appears full of hope in her yearbook picture, and with good reason. In the fall of 1921, she would move to New York City and begin her studies at Columbia University. Columbia University was an exciting place to be. Many of its professors were world-renowned experts in their fields, it had a beautiful urban campus close to the Hudson River, and students and professors from all over the world came to study and teach there. Among these professors were Clarence H. White and Arthur W. Dow, both important leaders in New York City's art world. They would introduce Margaret to the tools that would eventually bring her fortune and acclaim. And they would change the way she saw the world.

This is Margaret's senior high school photo in 1921. Listed next to her picture were the organizations and teams she was a part of, including the New School Song Committee, the Drama Club, and the swimming team.

TWO

Smokestacks on the Horizon

Margaret entered Columbia with her heart set on studying reptiles and amphibians. Her interest in cold-blooded creatures had stayed with her throughout her high school years. Over the course of her time in college, she continued to study the animal world, eventually graduating from Cornell University with a degree in herpetolgy. However, by starting college in New York City, Margaret accidentally found herself in the heart of America's art scene. Margaret's connection with the art world was initially slight in terms of the time she spent studying with with artists and photographers. Yet the effect her art and photography teachers at Columbia had on her would prove, in a matter of years, to be crucial to her development as a photographer.

New York was buzzing with new ideas about how to make photographs look more like paintings. Many photographers longed to have their work be seen as art. They considered themselves to be different from those who simply recorded visual facts. They wanted their photographs to be filled with the soul of whatever they photographed. These photographers were called Pictorialists.

Margaret's photography teacher, Clarence H. White, was a founder of the Pictorialist movement in photography. His views on composition were inspired in part by the work of the American artist James Whistler. Whistler had become famous for using rich colors and simple, bold shapes to create a romantic mood in the viewer. White achieved a similar effect by shooting slightly out of focus, blurring his camera lens with petroleum jelly, and by using natural light, especially at dawn or dusk.

White's students would experiment with all of these techniques but were able to develop their own styles. His student Dorothea Lange later became famous for her pictures of Americans experiencing poverty

Nocturne: Blue and Gold: Old Battersea Bridge **is an example of the type of painting Pictorialist photographers admired. Painted by James Whistler, it uses simple, bold forms and a limited range of tones to capture a romantic mood.**

and drought. Another, Margaret Watkins, became an assistant teacher at the school. Her successful career as a commercial photographer may have inspired Margaret to seek work in the same arena.

While Margaret only studied photography with White for two hours a week during the spring of 1922, the lessons she learned from him were seared on her brain and would reveal themselves in all of her work. It was as if the world was made out of hidden patterns and harmonies, and Margaret's job was to reveal them.

Through her studies in photography, Margaret made friends with a fellow Columbia student, Ralph Steiner. When Steiner looked back on his time studying with White, he said that White "painted with the camera." Steiner did not feel the same need to blur his photographs. He was more attracted to hard-edged forms that could be found in city landscapes, such as the spheres and cones of water towers, rectangular windows lit up at nighttime, or the lines of telegraph wires and poles. His love of precise geometric shapes would eventually affect Margaret as well.

Arthur Wesley Dow, another teacher of Margaret's at Columbia, also influenced her ideas about design. In his lectures he would explain how Japanese ink paintings and color woodcut prints use light and dark colors to create a sense of depth. He wanted his students to focus on arranging beautiful patterns of lines and shapes instead of telling a story.

A HELPING HAND

In January of 1922, Margaret's father died of a stroke. It was a huge loss for her. She had admired him greatly and had relied on him for advice and support. Unfortunately, as Margaret's biographer Vicki Goldberg writes, "She never had a chance to mourn his death . . . too much responsibility fell immediately on her shoulders." With her father gone, she was uncertain how she would be able to continue with her studies.

Photography's Varied Roles

When photography became popular after its invention in the mid-1800s, it was used mainly for portraits. As today, people loved to be able to see a permanent reflection of themselves, and they treasured having pictures of family and friends to put on their walls and tables. But while most professional photographers made their living taking portraits, others sought to record newsworthy events, places, and people. Mathew Brady photographed the Civil War, and Edward S. Curtis photographed the native peoples of the United States. When advertisers began to use photographs to sell their products, they often favored women photographers to shoot their advertisements. The thinking behind this was that because women made up the majority of the people who shopped, a woman photographer would better understand how to produce images that would attract shoppers to buy more.

For many decades, photographers had to rely on taking portraits, working for newspapers, or working for advertising agencies in order to make a living. The public was not ready to accept their work as an art-form worthy of the prices for which paintings could sell. Margaret was fortunate to meet teachers who dreamed of the day when photographs would take their place in museums alongside paintings, drawings, and sculptures. She used the tools they gave to her to create photographs that worked as advertising images, as photojournalism, and as art, and that would end up not only in magazines but also, decades later, in museums.

Her father had never made much money from his work, in spite of all the inventions he had produced. Without his income, Margaret had no way of paying for the following year's tuition for Columbia University.

Luckily, the Mungers, who were family friends of the Whites, offered Margaret a scholarship to study at the University of Michigan in Ann Arbor. Margaret would not forget the great favor. More than twenty years later, she dedicated her book *Shooting the Russian War* to one of the Mungers.

Margaret was excited about attending the University of Michigan, as it had a strong program in natural sciences. She still had a fascination with snakes and a love of the outdoors. In the summer between attending Columbia and Michigan, she worked as a camp counselor. At camp she started her first photography business, selling pictures of the surroundings to the campers. Her love of the outdoors and her love of photography were starting to come together.

Margaret is pictured here at the University of Michigan. It was the second of five universities she would attend before earning her degree in herpetology from Cornell University in 1927.

At the University of Michigan in the late fall of 1922, Margaret found a special friend with whom she felt a real bond. His name was Everett Chapman, and he was a senior who was studying electrical engineering. He was serious about his work, which reminded Margaret of her father, but he also had a great sense of humor. They read out loud to each other, hunted for snakes in the woods, and danced together. Chappie, as his friends called Everett, was an experienced amateur photographer who helped Margaret with lighting and developing techniques.

Chappie was not the only person at the University of Michigan to support Margaret's interest in photography. Joe Vlack, her colleague on the school yearbook, encouraged Margaret to approach photography with a sense of adventure and took her up on top of the roof of the engineering building to shoot pictures. Her zoology professor also aided her. He asked

Flappers Change the Rules

World War I had changed life for millions of people. Women were doing many jobs that used to be done by men only because so many men had to go off to fight in the war. By the 1920s, many young women in Europe and the United States had adopted a new style of dressing and new attitude. They felt comfortable doing things that were once thought to be unladylike, such as driving cars, riding bicycles, and dancing wild new dances such as the Charleston. Many of them, including Margaret, wore their hair in short bobs and dressed in skirts that came to just below the knee. These rebellious women were called flappers.

her to help him enlarge some of his pictures and arranged for her to work in the university's museum printing negatives. He suggested that she write a children's book of nature stories that her photographs would illustrate. This idea would stay on Margaret's mind for many years.

Around this time Margaret's mother revealed to her that she and her father had hidden the fact that he was Jewish. Margaret was very upset that this information was kept from her. For a while it made her anxious about her identity. According to her brother Roger's recollections, her mother chose to tell the family once the climate of anti-Semitism, or hostility toward Jews, had lessened in the United States.

Everett Chapman's passionate interest in science and photography captivated Margaret.

TEMPTING FATE

At the age of eighteen, Margaret could envision one career for herself in herpetology and one in photography. But she was only a sophomore in college, and her professional life was not her immediate concern. What was on her mind all the time was Chappie. After a few months of deepening romance, they decided to get married.

Margaret and Chappie went to a jeweler and bought a gold nugget from which Chappie made a wedding ring for Margaret. But when he hammered on it one last time to perfect the fit, the ring split in two. Ignoring this omen of trouble ahead, Margaret and Chappie proceeded to get married on Friday, June 13, 1923, one day before Margaret's nineteenth birthday. In trying to prove that they were not superstitious people, they seemed to be inviting bad luck.

In the first half of the twentieth century, it was not unusual for a nineteen-year-old woman to be married. Yet no matter how prepared Margaret was for the responsibility of marriage, she was not prepared for the possessiveness of her mother-in-law.

On her honeymoon with Chappie, a time that newlywed couples usually spend alone celebrating their marriage, Chappie's mother came to visit them in the cottage they had rented on the shores of Lake Michigan. One day when Chappie was out of the house, she told Margaret that she felt Minnie had gained a son and that she had lost a son, and that she never wanted to see Margaret again. Margaret immediately left the cabin and walked 17 miles (27 kilometers) in search of Chappie to tell him what had happened.

Margaret tried to make things work. She spent a year living with Chappie at Purdue University in Indiana, where he taught and she continued her studies. After a little more than two years had passed, they found that Chappie's mother was still unreasonably jealous of the marriage. Margaret and Chappie decided that they could not have the child they wanted under such conditions and soon realized they should divorce. While they had experienced some bouts of passion in the relationship, their inner lives were more oriented toward their intellectual and artistic passions than toward emotions. This made it easier for them to remain on friendly terms and continue to see each other occasionally.

Later in life, Margaret reflected on Chappie's mother. "As I look back," Margaret wrote, "I believe this beautiful rather tragic woman was the greatest single influence in my life. I am grateful to her because, all unknowing, she opened the door to a more spacious life than I could have ever dreamed." Chappie's mother had interfered with the traditional role of wife and mother Margaret could have performed and exposed her to the opportunity of making it on her own.

A PROFESSION COMES INTO VIEW

Margaret moved to Cleveland, Ohio, after separating from Chappie. She lived with her mother and younger brother Roger, who had relocated there after Joseph's death, and took classes at Case Western Reserve University for two semesters. In the fall of 1926, Margaret transferred to Cornell University in Ithaca, New York. She liked to tell people she chose Cornell because of the waterfalls that were on campus, but it also had much to offer her in terms of her interest in herpetology. She continued to use her photography to help her earn money, this time by taking pictures of the students and buildings on Cornell's beautiful campus.

A graduate of Cornell who saw one of Margaret's pictures was struck by its quality and made a bold suggestion to her. He thought that Margaret

Margaret's photograph of the train trestle, with Cleveland's Terminal Tower peeking under the right arch, echoes Whistler's painting of the Battersea Bridge.

should go to New York City to find out if there were opportunities for her in the field of architectural photography. Architectural photography, a new field at that time, documented the buildings that were being erected because of the nation's booming economy.

Margaret thought getting an opinion from someone at a New York City architectural firm would be a good idea. Only a true professional would know whether her work would appeal to business clients. She traveled to New York during spring break in March of 1927 to visit an architect named Benjamin Moscowitz, who had been recommended to her by a Cornell graduate. She met him just as he was leaving his office. He seemed to ignore what she said to him as he rushed to the elevator on the way to his train home. Before the elevator came, Margaret took out her photographs and caught his eye with her accomplished pictures of the Cornell campus.

"Did you take these?" he asked. Yes, she answered, that was what she had been trying to express. Moscowitz was very impressed. He skipped his train and invited Margaret into his office to discuss her work, telling her that her pictures were so strong that she could get work from any architectural firm in the country. With this vote of confidence, Margaret headed back to Cleveland. Moscowitz's praise likely helped her become more certain that photography was the best career choice for her, and that her interest in herpetology would have to take a back seat.

Margaret needed to return to Cleveland in order to finalize her divorce, but she also thought of Cleveland as a good place to begin her career, as it was a thriving industrial center. Especially gripping to her were the steel mills of the Flats, the area of Cleveland clustered around the Cuyahoga River. As Margaret recalled, "To me, fresh from college with a camera over my shoulder, the Flats were a photographic paradise. The smokestacks ringing the horizon were the giants of an unexplored world, guarding the secrets and wonder of the steel mills. When, I wondered, would I get inside those slab-sided coffin-black buildings with their mysterious unpredictable flashes of light leaking out the edges?"

THREE

The Fire Alight

One of the first things Margaret did when she got to Cleveland was change her last name from Chapman to Bourke-White, thus incorporating her mother's maiden name with her father's last name. It had a snappy sound and made her stand out from all the other Whites of the world.

Bourke-White figured that if Cleveland's wealthy would pay her to photograph their mansions and estates, she would be able to finance her pictures of their factories and smokestacks. She also offered her pictures to magazines and newspapers, knowing that they would expose her to a wider audience. Her wise plan worked by chance.

In her travels from office to office showing her portfolio to potential clients, Bourke-White would pass through Cleveland's public square. She did not normally carry her camera around and take pictures on these trips. One day, however, she saw a sight in the square that made her dash into the nearest camera store. A preacher was standing on a soapbox and sermonizing with arms outstretched, but the pigeons in the park were his only audience. Bourke-White just had to take a picture of this curious sight.

The clerk in the camera store was trusting enough to let Bourke-White borrow one of the store's cameras, and she ran back to the square. She tossed a few peanuts in front of the preacher so that the birds that had since flown off would again gather in front of him and then snapped away. Her picture charmed the Cleveland Chamber of Commerce so much that it bought the photograph to use for the cover of its monthly magazine and asked her to take more pictures.

In this picture of Bourke-White's, the preacher appears to be giving his sermon to the pigeons in the square.

A DIFFICULT ART

Bourke-White had found a new client, but more importantly, she had discovered a new teacher and friend. When Bourke-White went back to the camera store, she found herself studying the kind, luminous face of Alfred Hall Bemis, the clerk who had loaned her the camera. Fittingly, she would come to know him as "Beme."

Bemis was an experienced photographer who had a wealth of advice to offer Bourke-White about everything to do with lighting, shooting, and developing photographs. In addition, he was a source of encouragement and support, more than ready to spend long hours helping her find solutions to the technical problems her pictures posed. Taking photographs was generally much more complicated than it is today, and Bourke-White felt lucky to have Bemis's expertise.

While the invention of the Kodak and Brownie cameras around the turn of the century had allowed the amateur photographer to take snapshots and have them professionally developed, the professional photographer who wanted complete control over the process had to invest in costly machinery and chemicals. The images were recorded either on a treated glass plate or on celluloid, a chemically coated plastic. While smaller amateur cameras could take multiple pictures, professional cameras of the 1920s often required reloading after every shot. A curtain had to cover the camera and photographer when she took out the film, or else light would hit the glass or celluloid, and the picture would be overdeveloped, ruining the image.

The bulky cameras Bourke-White often used were heavy enough that they needed to be supported on a three-legged stand called a tripod.

Margaret liked to dress fashionably, even when shooting outdoors in conditions that were not favorable for high heels.

Unlike most photographers of today, who peer with one eye through a tiny viewfinder at their subject, Bourke-White looked down with both eyes into the glass field of her camera. The image appeared much wider than in today's miniature cameras, which allowed her to compose her photograph with an idea of what it would look like after she had printed it.

The image recorded on the film or glass would be taken to a darkroom, which was a lab that had been sealed off from outside light. The tiniest amount of light would ruin the film. There the film would be placed in a chemical bath that would fix the image into negatives, or images that had the reverse tones of the original. A projector would then beam light through the negative onto chemically treated paper. This paper was placed into the chemical bath to be developed into a positive image. The process was complicated and continues to challenge the photographers of today, who still use essentially the same steps for film photography.

CAPTURING MOLTEN STEEL

By the winter of 1928, Bourke-White's photography business was taking off. Architects, department stores, banks, and magazines were requiring her skills. She was earning enough money to buy a flashy wardrobe and put a down payment on a used car, which she named "Patrick." She had outfits made in colors that matched the colors of her camera curtains. And she was able to pay Earl Leiter, an expert developer, to take her celluloid and develop it into beautiful prints.

One day while having lunch with Bemis, a question came into Bourke-White's mind. "Aren't the presidents of banks on the boards of directors of industries, and vice versa?" She was thinking in particular of John Sherwin, the head of the Union Trust bank. Bourke-White had photographed a live bull, which schoolboys had raised, snorting as he stood in the huge lobby of Sherwin's bank. Margaret wasn't clear about what the image was supposed to symbolize, but Sherwin's bank had been very happy with the photograph and ordered 450 prints to send to newspapers and to schools.

Bourke-White had also photographed his wife's garden. Maybe Sherwin would be the right person to introduce her to Elroy Kulas, the head of the Otis Steel mills that she had been longing to photograph. Bemis thought he would be. As it turned out, Sherwin did not understand why a "pretty young girl should want to take pictures in a dirty steel mill," but he wrote a letter of introduction for Bourke-White to take to Kulas anyway.

When Bourke-White met with Kulas, she surprised him with her passion for the steel industry. She told him she was convinced that

The might of American industry is displayed in this photograph by Bourke-White. Note the men dwarfed by the smokestacks towering above them.

industrial forms were beautiful "because they were never designed to be beautiful. They had a simplicity of line that came from their direct application to a purpose." Bourke-White felt it was her job to capture the unconscious, hidden beauty of the steel mills.

Kulas was concerned about the dangers she would face in the mills from the fumes, heat, and heavy machinery. But Bourke-White's passionate speech made him feel that her photos could be used to promote the steel mills, should she successfully photograph them. No one had ever taken pictures of a steel mill operation before, at least not to Kulas and Bourke-White's knowledge.

At last he gave her the go-ahead. Bourke-White had permission to visit the mill at any time, day or night. She was ecstatic.

Luckily for Bourke-White, the next thing Kulas did was to go on vacation for five months. It took her almost that long to get the photographs of which she had been dreaming. The biggest challenge she faced was lighting. Although the steel grew very bright when it was heated and poured into molds, the mills themselves were not brightly lit. Bourke-White would have to use flashes in order to illuminate the mill. This would prove to be a challenge, as timed electronic flashes had not been invented at this time. Illuminating dark scenes was done with flash powder, a dangerous chemical that was hard to control.

Another challenge Bourke-White faced was the heat of the steel, which threatened to burn her and her camera and damage the film. When she first visited the mill, these difficulties did not faze her. Bemis remembered her "as delighted as a kid with a Fourth of July firecracker" as she danced and sang through the mill in her high heels and skirt. But when she and Leiter developed her first photographs, the glowing steel she had seen through her camera was barely there on the print. She needed more light.

Bemis helped her find a solution for her problem. A traveling salesman by the name of H. F. Jackson was passing through town on his way to Hollywood, where he was planning to demonstrate the effects of the huge magnesium flares his company had developed. When Bemis told Jackson about Bourke-White's lighting problem, he volunteered to use some of them for her project. Now they were able to capture the pouring of the steel, but the printing paper was not capturing the beauty they could see in the negatives. Again, a contact of Bemis's came to the rescue. Charlie Bolwell, a representative of photographic paper companies, was an expert in developing photographs. He showed Bourke-White techniques that would help her, such as dipping her hand in the chemical bath to warm up the underexposed areas of the prints.

Finally Bourke-White, Leiter, and her cast of technical angels produced the photographs they wanted—shots of glowing metal, lurching cranes, and helmet-clad steelworkers surrounded by sparks from their blowtorches. Kulas loved her pictures and immediately expressed an interest in buying them. The pictures were printed in a privately published booklet called *The Story of Steel* and were published in a number of Midwestern newspapers.

Bourke-White records in her autobiography that she was often thinking of her father during this time. She wished that he had been able to see the photographic miracle she had achieved. As she wrote, "My love for industrial form and pattern was his unconscious gift."

Before Bourke-White took this photograph, few people had seen the inner workings of a steel mill.

A WIDER STAGE

One day in 1929, Bourke-White received a telegram from Henry Luce, the publisher of *Time*, the popular and influential weekly news magazine. Her pictures of Cleveland's steel mills had impressed him, and he thought she would be the perfect photographer for *Fortune*, the new magazine he was starting. At first she had doubts about going to New York to meet Luce. The photographs in *Time* magazine were mostly of people, especially of those in politics, and Bourke-White was devoted to the machine.

After thinking about the telegram for two days, she decided to take a chance and go to New York to hear Luce's ideas for the new magazine. As luck would have it, Luce wanted to create a magazine devoted to the Machine Age, which was what the nation's industrial boom was being called. The magazine's photographs and stories would show how all the

Black Thursday Blues

On Thursday, October 24, 1929, the New York Stock Exchange crashed when stock prices fell, causing brokers to panic and sell some thirteen million shares. Millions of Americans lost most or all of the money they had invested, many banks that had lent people money went bankrupt, and many businesses lost their line of credit. As businesses were left without money to operate, many workers were laid off, and millions of people became unemployed. Ironically, Bourke-White was photographing a bank vault when news of the crash spread.

different parts of industrial production, distribution, and marketing fit together. Readers of *Fortune* would then have a better understanding of the relationship between machines, factories, factory workers, businesses, and business owners.

Bourke-White was excited. She felt that the magazine would give photography new opportunities and challenges. In fact, she later recalled, "I was so happy I was almost afraid to walk across the street, for fear I would be run over before I had a chance to embark on this wonderful new life." Her new work would have her collaborating closely with *Fortune*'s editors, who were responsible for generating ideas for its content and reviewing the submissions of its authors, photographers, and illustrators. She looked forward to working with people whose vision of industry was so close to her own, on a stage wide enough to include the whole of North America and eventually the world.

FOUR

Machine-Age Adventures

Bourke-White began to work on the first issue of *Fortune* in the summer of 1929 and moved to New York City the next summer. But she would not stay long in New York, as her work for *Fortune* demanded that she travel all over the country, focusing her lens on American business. In her first year, she would travel all over the United States, taking photographs of a wide variety of industries, including glass-blowing, watch making, toy making, meatpacking, and news printing.

In factories that made sewing machines, nurseries that raised orchids, and fisheries that froze their catch, Bourke-White captured the nation's amazing productivity. With her passion and commitment to getting the best picture possible, she was not fazed by some of the difficulties industrial photography presented her. She stood on top of a mountain of fish, endured the fumes of dead pigs, and even snowshoed in the freezing cold, all in order to get the perfect shots for the magazine.

Late in the fall of 1929, Bourke-White was assigned to do a story on the construction of New York City's Chrysler Building for *Fortune*'s series of articles on skyscrapers. This building, rising 1,046 feet (319 meters) in the air, was a masterpiece of Art Deco architecture. It was Bourke-White's job to take pictures of the tower of the Chrysler Building, which rose 125 feet (38.1 m) above the top of the building. Amazingly, working at such an incredible height did not scare her. As she put it, "I have a God-given sense of balance and also a great deal of practice in my childhood. My sister Ruth and I had a pact to walk the entire

Bourke-White's assistant Oscar Graubner photographed Margaret shooting from one of the gargoyles of the Chrysler Building in Manhattan.

distance to school and back on the thin edges of fences. It was a point of honor to dismount only for crossroads and brooks."

Yet the effort she put into keeping her balance hundreds of feet in the freezing air took a toll on her. At the end of one particularly exhausting workday, she found she could not make the step from the curb into a taxicab, and fell and scraped her legs. "I am often impressed," she reflected later, "with how the human body will store its little infirmities until there is time to deal with them." In other words, Bourke-White's body needed a chance to collapse but chose a safe moment to do it, causing her to fall a foot or two instead of hundreds of feet.

AN OFFICE ON HIGH

Bourke-White decided she wanted her office to be on the Chrysler Building's sixty-first floor, from which stainless-steel, eagle-headed

The Fearless Sky Walkers

Many of the ironworkers and steelworkers who built the skyscrapers of New York City were Mohawk Indians who came from reservations in northern New York and Canada, to help with the construction. Mohawks continued to cultivate their skills since their grace and agility were first noticed on a construction site in 1886. They seemed to have no fear of heights while walking across narrow beams hundreds of feet above the ground. While working on the buildings, Mohawks would often communicate using a sign language they had invented because other workers were too far away to be heard.

gargoyles jutted out over the streets below. Her income from *Fortune* was not enough to pay the rent, so she began to do advertising photography as well. She started with two companies, Buick autos and Goodyear tires. Her work soon expanded, and she ended up taking pictures that would be used in ads for everything from chewing gum to airplanes. More important, she was able to pay the rent for her dream office.

Bourke-White had the designer and illustrator John Vassos create her studio space in the Art Deco style for which he was well known. He used aluminum, wood, and glass to make clean, strong lines and open spaces. Bourke-White loved showing people her huge fish tank, which was set into a wall. Once, she even had a barber come up to her office and shave her friend's beard on the terrace next to her studio, on which she kept two pet alligators. She was so in love with the space that she wished she could live there, but only the night janitor was allowed to do that. She applied for the job but was turned down. In order to get the most out of the space, she would often stay up all night in her office.

Bourke-White excelled at aerial photography. Note the Chrysler building rising up behind the right wing of the airplane.

While Bourke-White was learning important lighting and color-photography techniques in advertising, she greatly preferred her work for *Fortune*. For her, advertising used words and images that gave products powers they didn't really have. She also disliked how much money companies spent on making their products seem better than their competitors'. For one assignment, she and her assistant spent hours making fake mud through which a fake wooden tire would run. Thousands of dollars were spent on pretending the picture demonstrated the tread of a real tire, with "the crispest, most 'convincing' tire track the nation's motorists had ever seen," Bourke-White recalled in disgust.

PICTURES AS A PASSPORT

In late June of 1930, *Fortune* sent Bourke-White overseas to document Germany's industrial expansion. Bourke-White proposed going on to the Soviet Union after her work in Germany was done. No U.S. photographers or writers had been officially allowed by the Soviet Union to cover what was happening within its borders. The country had a mysterious power, especially for Bourke-White, who loved to explore the hidden.

When Bourke-White applied for her visa at the Soviet embassy in Washington, D.C., she was told that her pictures would be her passport. The Soviet official she met with thought her photographs had a Soviet style to them. Like Bourke-White, many Soviet artists were celebrating what they felt was the uplifting power of the Machine Age. Their posters and photographs used bold gestures and dynamic diagonal lines to show the interaction between mighty machines and equally mighty workers. The work of Aleksandr Rodchenko modeled this approach.

Bourke-White was in Germany for over a month waiting for permission to enter the Soviet Union. In the meantime she had gotten into trouble with the German authorities, who suspected that she was taking pictures of German shipbuilding and other industries in order to spy on the country. The professionalism of her portfolio of U.S. industrial sites convinced them she was a photographer. Her photographs had become a passport out of jail, at the very least.

When permission from the Soviets did finally come, Bourke-White prepared to enter a country lacking many of the conveniences she was used to as an American. The Soviet Union was suffering from a famine, so she stuffed canned food into her luggage, which was already bursting with photographic equipment. She was heading to a country that was young and struggling, and she had no idea what kind of treatment she could expect from its government.

A Daring Feat

In 1932, Amelia Earhart became the first woman to fly a plane solo over the Atlantic Ocean. She departed from Harbor Grace in Newfoundland, Canada, on May 20 and arrived in Londonderry, Ireland, on May 21, 14 hours and 56 minutes later. She had originally planned to land in Paris, but poor weather conditions forced her to land in an Irish cow pasture.

Earhart once wrote a letter to Bourke-White after seeing her photograph of the George Washington Bridge under construction. She complimented Bourke-White for her accomplished picture, saying that it showed the power that was hidden in women.

The Soviet Union's communist government had grown out of the socialist ideas of the nineteenth-century German philosophers Karl Marx and Friedrich Engels, who popularized a version of socialism they called Communism. The communists believed in a classless society in which there would be no rich, middle class, or poor. Property would be owned by the state, and wealth would be distributed equally. Workers would share in the ownership of businesses, which would prevent business profits from going into the hands of a few rich owners and shareholders. People who had previously been poor and illiterate would receive free education, political representation, a living wage, and free health care.

The Russian Vladimir Lenin thought the best way to achieve this type of society was through a revolution led by the proletariat. The proletariat was defined as those who did not own the businesses in which they worked, making money primarily by selling their labor. A more common term for the proletariat is the working class. With the Russian Revolution in 1918, the proletariat defeated the ruling class of Russia, and communist ideas had a chance to be put into practice. Lenin also formed the Communist International, or Comintern, to promote revolutions in other countries.

In the United States these ideas received a mixed reception. Some Americans admired the communists' attempt to improve the lives of workers. But many Americans disagreed with communism. They felt that the United States' capitalistic democracy offered a freer way of life in which individuals and private corporations could compete for profits. The need to offer better services than one's competitors would force people and companies to be innovative. Competition would breed new products and even new industries, which would in turn create more jobs and more wealth. This was unlikely to happen in a nation rooted in communism, according to its capitalist critics, and the United States should therefore work to stop its spread.

However, as Bourke-White noticed when she was in the Soviet Union, the American opposition to communist ideas did not get in the way of American companies making a profit in the Soviet Union. As she later wrote, "The role played by American industrialists in building up the Soviet Union cannot be overestimated." Engineers from U.S. companies were in the Soviet Union, helping to set up the assembly lines and build the ships, dams, and oil refineries Bourke-White was photographing. The Soviets relied on the United States for its technical advice and for its investment in huge new projects. In the end, ironically, the United States helped make the Soviet Union powerful enough to compete with the United States for global dominance.

This photograph is at once Bourke-White's portrait of the American engineer Hugh L. Cooper, and of the Soviet dam he helped to build across the Dnieper River in the Ukraine.

FIVE

Behind the Machine

When Bourke-White returned to the United States in the fall of 1930, she began work on her first book, *Eyes on Russia.* The book was widely celebrated, and people were especially captivated by Bourke-White's pictures. Bourke-White returned to the Soviet Union in 1931 and 1932 and was encouraged by these two trips. She felt that the Soviet people were more focused on controlling and applying the power of the new machines. In addition, she admired the way many Soviet women were entering the workforce without a sense of conflict between their homes and their jobs.

On the surface the Soviet Union's plan to update its industry in a rapid, five-year push was succeeding. The Soviet leader, Joseph Stalin, was in firm command of the government and was seen by many as capable of directing the transformation. But something atrocious was happening away from the eyes and ears of foreigners such as Bourke-White, who were not able to travel independently and investigate the country freely.

Bourke-White did not know that the famine in the Ukraine, a republic in southwestern Soviet Union, was a result of the demand of Stalin and his comrades that farmers drastically increase their production of grain for use by the state. The Soviet government deliberately set quotas for Ukrainian grain production that were too high. This left little grain for the Ukrainians to use for themselves. Without enough of their basic foodstuff, millions died. Stalin's objective in raising the grain quotas was in part to crush the Ukrainian movement for independence from the Soviet Union. He also wanted to quash the Ukrainian farmers' resistance to working on collective farms, which were controlled by the state. His brutal means ensured success.

The Russian textile worker in this picture of Bourke-White's seems secondary to the beauty of the sweeping diagonal of the spools of thread.

Bourke-White's chaperones also prevented her from finding out about the gulags, the forced-labor camps that were completing some of Stalin's biggest projects, such as digging canals and clearing forests. In these camps, people had no control over how long they worked or what work they did. In the 1960s, the Russian writer and former gulag prisoner Aleksandr Solzhenitsyn wrote of these camps, "Who, except prisoners, would have worked at logging ten hours a day, in addition to marching four miles through the woods in predawn darkness and the same distance back at night, in a temperature of minus 20, and knowing in a year no other rest days than May 1 and November 7?" When his manuscript about the gulags was discovered by the Soviet authorities in 1974, they forced him to leave the country.

Bourke-White would gain a better sense of who Stalin really was when she took his portrait during World War II. In the meantime, she continued to praise the Soviet Union and on her last trip even made two motion pictures about its peoples' achievements. The films were a disappointment to Bourke-White. "I did all the wrong things: used big cameras, big films, big tripods. I composed each scene with lengthy care and took innumerable static views, forgetting that the important word in motion pictures is *motion*." Nonetheless, the films did make their way into the world. In fact, a reporter friend of Bourke-White's told her years later that he had seen one in a little theater deep in the Brazilian countryside.

A CHANGE IN FOCUS

In the summer of 1934, the editors of *Fortune* had a new type of assignment for Bourke-White. Instead of covering the growth and the products of U.S. industries, they now needed her to cover the crisis U.S. farmers were facing. A great drought had taken hold of a wide area of the Great

Plains in the American Midwest. Strong winds were whipping up soil from the dry fields. Huge dust storms were covering whole towns, and the dust was creeping into everything. Since the land was not able to sustain crops, and the dust was impossible to escape, many families left the region and headed west to escape what was becoming known as the Dust Bowl.

Bourke-White chartered a pilot and his tiny, old two-seater plane to fly over Nebraska, North and South Dakota, and other states suffering

The parched land and stunted corn of the Great Plains was a bleak sight. Drought and storms afflicted the agricultural center of the United States during the 1930s, adding more suffering to a nation already beaten down by the poor economic conditions of the Great Depression.

from the drought. "I had never seen landscapes like those through which we flew," she later wrote. "Below us the ghostly patchwork of half-buried corn, and the rivers of sand which should have been free-running streams." The land was devastated, but it was the suffering that the drought had caused the region's families that affected Bourke-White the most. Their helplessness touched her deeply. What could they do for their suffering animals, many of which were choking from the dust and dying of starvation?

The trip to the Dust Bowl changed Bourke-White. Before, she was focused on the glory of the machine. The people who operated the machines were useful to give a sense of scale, showing how huge the machines were in the pictures she took. But now she saw the faces of suffering human individuals and felt a need to document them and tell their stories.

Few Markets for the Goods

The Great Depression, which began with the stock market crash of 1929 and ended with World War II, was a very difficult period for people all over the world. In the United States during the 1920s, factories were producing goods at a rapid pace, but the workers didn't earn enough money to afford to buy all of the products made. With the surplus goods remaining in company storehouses, the companies were not earning enough money to pay their workers. Millions of people lost their jobs, and the struggle to find work, food, and even shelter became a battle for many.

Bourke-White had been wildly successful at showing the dramatic rise of industry in the Machine Age, when hundreds of skyscrapers shot into the air, and shiny new automobiles sped on gleaming roads beneath them. But could her camera depict the drama of the human beings who had built the towers and the cars? Would her images be able to convey unspoken thoughts and feelings? She was passionate to find out and sought a way to test her skills.

In order to explore human issues, Bourke-White needed to change format. She wanted to do an extensive investigation of individual lives and the forces that affected them. Her advertising photography business was bringing in a lot of money, but it was too demanding of her time, and she had completely lost patience with the exaggeration her clients used in selling their products. Furthermore, *Fortune*, with its short articles and focus on businesspeople, would not be the right place for her new project. She decided she needed to stop her advertising work and write a book.

Even though Bourke-White had already written a book and a number of magazine articles, she did not think of herself as a writer. She wanted to find an author whose writing would interact with the book's images. The only other thing she knew was that he or she should be "earnest about understanding America."

About two weeks after committing herself to this project, she heard that an author named Erksine Caldwell was looking for a photographer. Caldwell had gained fame for a controversial novel he had written in 1932 about the American South called *Tobacco Road*, which had become a successful Broadway play. Some doubted that Caldwell's description of the poverty and suffering in the South was accurate. He wanted to write a nonfiction book that would document in words and pictures the reality behind his stories.

DOCUMENTING LIFE IN THE SOUTH

Bourke-White and Caldwell had trouble getting started on the book. Because she had decided to stop doing advertising photography, she needed to close down her office. She also had a commitment to *Fortune*. Caldwell grew so impatient to begin that Bourke-White flew to Georgia to convince him of her sincere intention to work on the book. They began in the summer of 1936, driving all over the South, interviewing individuals and families in the fields and in their homes.

Caldwell's manner impressed Bourke-White. He had a way of gaining the trust of strangers. Bourke-White felt this was partly because he was able to speak to them using their local accent. While Caldwell would talk, Bourke-White would shoot photos, sometimes with a camera on remote control. She hoped that she would be able to catch people at the moment that best revealed the emotions behind what they were saying to Caldwell.

The real success of Bourke-White and Caldwell's project was the way the photographs helped to argue the points that Caldwell was making in the book. He was strongly against the system of tenant farming and sharecropping, which were keeping millions of Southerners in poverty and increasing tension between blacks and whites. In the system of tenant farming, a farmer would grow cotton and other crops on the fields he rented from a landlord. He would pay the landlord rent with a portion of what he had raised and with cash from selling the crops.

Many poor families could not afford to properly wallpaper or insulate their homes and used pages of newspapers and magazines instead.

Sharecroppers, most of whom were black, were a step below tenant farmers in that they were paid primarily by getting a share of the crops they had farmed. The value of these crops was set by the landlord. Many of the tenant farmers and sharecroppers could not read. Landlords would take advantage of this by telling the tenant farmers and sharecroppers that they were owed less than they deserved, or that they were in debt to the landlord for more than the true amount. Demanding to see a written record would be useless, because the farmers wouldn't be able to read it. In addition, the landlords charged inflated prices for supplies in the local stores as a way of keeping the tenant farmers and sharecroppers poor, and threatened them with violence if they complained. Whites would sometimes murder black sharecroppers if they felt threatened by them, usually by lynching them, leaving their bodies hanging from trees as a warning to others.

In Bourke-White's pictures, viewers who did not live in the South could now see up close the terrible conditions in which tenant farmers and sharecroppers lived. Their homes were falling apart, their clothes were torn, their bodies were ragged from malnutrition and exhaustion, and their faces were furrowed with pain.

In her autobiography, Bourke-White remembered one child she met named Begonia, who had a twin sister. Begonia would take turns going to school with her sister, because there was only one pair of shoes and one coat for the both of them. All around their house were pages of advertisements torn from magazines that were being used for insulation,

Rescuing the Economy

In 1933, President Roosevelt rapidly put in to place a number of new programs to help pull the country out of the Great Depression. These programs increased both the size of the federal government and its influence on people's lives. Collectively, these programs were known as the New Deal. The government quickly enacted laws protecting workers' rights. Engineers and laborers rushed to start huge dam projects to increase the nation's energy supply. The Securities and Exchange Commission was created in order to regulate the stock market. Programs such as the Works Progress Administration helped employ skilled workers. With the establishment of Social Security, senior citizens were given a pension that could help support them if they had little or no savings. Historians continue to debate how helpful the New Deal was in rescuing the U.S. economy.

as the family could not afford plaster. "Begonia and her sister could look their walls over and find a complete range of shoes, jackets and coats. But never would they find that real coat and real pair of shoes that would take the second twin to school," Bourke-White later wrote.

Once, while driving down a country road, Bourke-White and Caldwell came across a chain gang and its captain working on the side of the road. Chain gangs are teams of prisoners who are chained together and taken out into the fields or onto roads to do supervised manual labor. The captain of the chain gang was watching over the prisoners carefully with his gun at the ready and would not give Bourke-White permission to take photographs of the men.

Caldwell had an idea. He would drive past the chain gang while Bourke-White took pictures out the back window. When the captain threatened to shoot out their tires, they had to abandon the plan. "Not too regretfully on my part," Bourke-White noted, "because photographs caught on the fly may serve as a record but they allow no chance for careful composition." With this comment Bourke-White revealed how different she was from other photographers working at the time, such as Weegee and Robert Capa. For them, recording real life was more important than getting a composed picture. Bourke-White would move in this direction, but it would take time. It was hard for her to exchange the sharp pictures that large cameras created for the quick response of smaller ones.

A BALANCING ACT

You Have Seen Their Faces, as Bourke-White and Caldwell titled their book, was published in 1937 to wide acclaim and helped awaken the movement to improve the lives of poor Southerners. The Philadelphia *Public Record* observed that the book alerted readers to a new kind of slavery. However, some critics felt that Bourke-White had taken the wrong approach in photographing her subjects. The people in Bourke-White's pictures seemed stiff, as if Bourke-White had asked them to pose in the most effective way possible. The problem was not that Bourke-White was creating a false image of her subjects, one in which she made them pose with expressions that did not show the way they felt. The problem was that with her heavy cameras and tripods, scenes that would have caught her eyes as spontaneous windows into people's feelings would then have to be frozen until she could get them on film.

Bourke-White and Caldwell were also criticized for the captions that appeared next to peoples' pictures. Bourke-White and Caldwell had written typical comments they thought the people in their book would make instead of quoting what they had actually said. The work of other well-known photographers of the time who documented poor farmers, including Dorothea Lange, Walker Evans, and Ben Shahn, is thought by many to be more respectful and less controlled than Bourke-White's photographs.

Bourke-White and Caldwell grew very close while working on their book. Caldwell wanted to marry Bourke-White, but she was afraid if she married him it would get in the way of her work, which was the most important thing in her life. She had a well-paying career that offered her opportunities to travel all over the world. How would being married fit with that life? Would her husband accompany her on her trips? If not, how would they hold on to their connection, when Bourke-White could be out of the country for months on assignment?

Bourke-White hoped that there would be a way to balance marriage and career. She and Caldwell had even dedicated *You Have Seen Their Faces* to Patricia, the name of the child they hoped to have someday.

THINKING OF FAMILY

Bourke-White's family was in a difficult position financially when her father died, but the family managed to make do. Her mother worked with the blind, and her sister was an administrator for the American Bar Association. Her little brother was just starting college, however, and he relied on Bourke-White to help him out. She was happy to but often had to juggle helping her brother and paying her own bills. Bourke-White frequently had to rely on her secretaries to deal with difficult financial matters, as she was often out of the city on assignment.

In the summer of 1936, Bourke-White's mother was taking summer classes at Columbia University. Bourke-White thought it would be a wonderful idea to take her mother on a plane trip that she was photographing for Eastern Airlines. Bourke-White loved to do aerial photography. Looking down on a city and photographing the airplanes that would fly beneath hers, she found a viewpoint few Americans had ever had. Her mother was thrilled by the idea of flying with her daughter. However, as soon as she announced the trip to her class, she had a heart attack and collapsed. Two days later, she died.

Bourke-White's feelings about her mother's death did not come to the surface easily. She was not as close to her mother as she was to her father, and she bore some resentment toward her for being so strict during her childhood. At the same time she respected her mother's commitment to teaching her children good values and to helping them be brave. She also admired her mother for her lifelong pursuit of learning.

Later, in Bourke-White's autobiography, she was able to look back and pay tribute to her mother. Though sorrowful at the death of her mother, Bourke-White thought that she had died in an appropriate way. As Bourke-White put it, Minnie had died with "eyes looking forward to an ever-expanding horizon, exploring still, even in the last conscious moment of her life."

SIX

Standing Her Ground

The year 1936 was a turning point in Bourke-White's life in a number of ways. At the age of thirty-two, she had decided to phase out advertising work and to cover social issues more in depth. She had lost her mother, and she had found a new love. Her fame had been growing steadily, and she even been named one of the ten most notable women in the United States.

Henry Luce, the publisher of *Time* and *Fortune*, wanted to capitalize on this fame. He had an idea for a new magazine he wanted to start, and he wanted Bourke-White to be its star photographer. The magazine was to be called *Life*, and it would make photographs the central part of its stories. *Life* would include features on politics and on business, as *Time* and *Fortune* did, but it would appeal to a broader range of readers by covering sporting events, fashion, travel, hobbies, science, and entertainment.

Luce realized that Americans had a thirst for stories told in a series of images and chose the photo- or picture-essay as the means to satisfy it.

Not only did Luce want to make Bourke-White *Life* magazine's star, he was also ready to bring her whole staff from her photography studio over to *Life*. In addition, he promised to give Bourke-White her own office, something he did not do for the other three staff photographers. Her staff made a valuable contribution to *Life*. One of them, Bourke-White's darkroom printer, Oscar Graubner, became chief of the

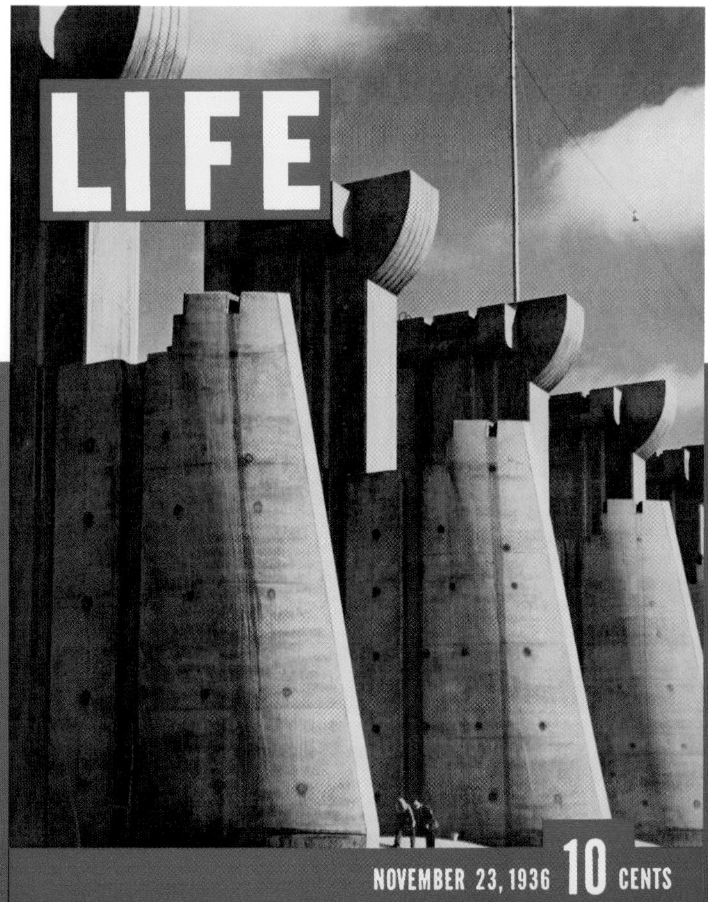

Bourke-White's photograph of the giant concrete sections of the Fort Peck Dam in Montana was the first image to grace the cover of *Life* magazine. *Life*'s first issue was published on November 23, 1936.

photo lab. He followed her practice of "printing black" with all of *Life*'s photographers. In this process, the entire image the photographer had captured on the film was developed, instead of an image that was cropped in the projector. The black border surrounding the image showed that the printer had "printed black," developing everything inside the black borders of the negative. By preserving what photographers had first seen in the camera, their creation was respected. It was then up to the editor to decide if the photograph would work as it was. Bourke-White's routinely did.

Bourke-White's first assignment was to cover the building of the Fort Peck Dam, a project of President Roosevelt's New Deal. Bourke-White journeyed to New Deal, Montana, a town on the Columbia River where the dam was being built. In addition to being the largest earth-filled dam in the world, the project was important because it was providing employment for workers who had been out of work for long stretches during the ongoing Depression.

Bourke-White returned from the assignment with pictures not only of the bold, abstract shape of the dam under construction, but also of the people who were building it. *Life*'s editors were surprised to see Bourke-White's photos of the nightlife of New Deal. They were used to seeing her photographs of machines and buildings, so her pictures of the bar patrons and dancers in the frontier town signaled a shift. One of the pictures they chose for the photo-essay on the dam was of people lined up against a bar, on top of which sat a four-year-old girl. Some readers were shocked, not knowing that the girl was the daughter of the waitress. *Life* was happy to have caused some controversy. It would help to sell the magazine.

BOURKE-WHITE GOES MUCKRAKING

One of Bourke-White's first stories for *Life* after her Fort Peck Dam story was about the corrupt mayor of Jersey City, Frank Hague. He was turning a blind eye to the child labor abuses happening in his city. Working in what were called "home industries," children were missing school in order to help their parents make paper lamp shades and artificial flowers. Working together, the families would earn just enough to pay the rent on housing that was falling apart. Bourke-White's job was to photograph children working in one of these homes in order to prove that child-labor laws were being broken under Mayor Hague's watch.

Bourke-White's strategy to get her photos and story was to make herself the mayor's pet reporter. In the spring of 1937, she covered a number of his speeches, jumping up to photograph him when he

Digging in the Dirt

In a speech in 1906, President Theodore Roosevelt complained about reporters who dug in the dirt, trying to stir up problems they could turn into sensational stories for their newspapers. He called these reporters muckrakers. The term lost its negative meaning in time and now means someone who tries hard to uncover the hidden truth. One famous photojournalist who wrote a muckraking book in 1890 about New York City's poor was Jacob Riis. His book was called *How the Other Half Lives*, and it helped better the living conditions of those living in New York's slums.

shouted things like, "I am the law!" or "I decide; I do; me!" Once Hague and the police thought she was a sympathetic presence at city hall, she took a detour to the "home industries" area to photograph the children working alongside their parents and grandparents. The police caught up with her and confiscated the film in her cameras. Little did they know that not long before, one of Bourke-White's assistants had started making his way back to *Life*'s offices with the film from one of the cameras that had captured the evidence of Hague's corruption.

Around this time Bourke-White's social conscience was also finding expression in her support of arts organizations such as the American Artists' Congress and the American Youth Congress. Two main aims of the American Artists' Congress were to speak out against Fascism (the political philosophy that supports control by a dictatorial leader who strictly regiments society and the economy and severely crushes political opposition) and to appeal for government support for the arts. Bourke-White's backing of these organizations would later come back to haunt her.

BUTTERFLIES IN THE ARCTIC

Bourke-White was thrilled when she saw the advance copy of *Life*'s first issue, which appeared on the newsstands in November of 1936. She wrote to one of the editors, "We're going to have a splendid time watching *Life* grow up. It has more possibilities than anything I can think of. I'm going to start raising caterpillars for some butterfly pictures soon. It delights me to think that even the herpetologist and entomologist who was folded away in a college diploma can come to *Life* also."

When butterflies emerge from their cocoons, they do not usually head for the Arctic, but that is what Bourke-White did in 1937. She managed to pack two trips in one, shooting photos for a corporate publication by the International Paper Company and accompanying the governor-general of Canada on a tour by ship of Canada's arctic regions. Her work for the International Paper Company, which was responsible for making the paper for many U.S. newspapers, was to a degree a return to her advertising work. However, while the corporate publication would promote the company to its investors, it would not be full of the exaggerated claims the ads Bourke-White once had to do were. Instead, the company asked her to photograph the story of paper. She followed the trees' journey from a forest in the far north of Quebec to a sawmill where their branches were cut off. After this they were sent down the river to the plant where they would be turned into the pulp that would make newsprint.

She had covered the company before for *Fortune*'s first issue, but as the art historian John Stomberg has observed, her approach was very

The speed and rhythmic pulse of industrial production fascinated Bourke-White.

different this time. She chartered a plane to capture from midair majestic pictures of logs floating in abstract forms down a river. She also photographed the people living in the mill towns up close, showing that her experiences in the Dust Bowl and in the South had truly impacted her. She wanted to show that the way people lived was a part of the paper they produced.

Bourke-White's trip accompanying Lord Tweedsmuir, the governor-general of Canada, was one of the most enjoyable she ever had. She brought along a number of chrysalises of the mourning cloak butterfly, as she was hoping to take pictures of them emerging from their sacs as butterflies. These pictures would go into the children's book she had been thinking of doing since she was at the University of Michigan. She taped the chrysalises to a rail on the ship's deck, and they managed to survive in the cold temperatures of the Arctic summer. The captain promised her he would stop the boat as soon as the butterflies started to emerge, so that she could hold her camera steady as she shot her pictures. Later, she flew in a tiny plane over the icy ranges of northernmost Canada for a *Life* feature about the Arctic Ocean. She sheltered herself from the cold in a special parka designed by an Inuit woman, with "caribou trimmed with white reindeer breast and a hood lined in wolverine fur."

THE TENSIONS BUILD

In the spring of 1938, Bourke-White and Caldwell traveled to Czechoslovakia to cover the tensions there. The Germans had recently invaded and occupied Austria, and many people were worried that Czechoslovakia would be next to fall because of its large German population.

Bourke-White and Caldwell found that the country was already affected by the German occupation of Austria. Many Jews, fearful of the Nazis, had immigrated to Czechoslovakia. In one town, the refugees had been thrown into jail. When Bourke-White and Caldwell asked the jailer why, he told them that there simply was no room for them anywhere else. He was so embarrassed by what his town had done that he let them out just after Bourke-White and Caldwell ended their visit with him.

Bourke-White felt that the pictures she took in Czechoslovakia, and the book *North of the Danube* that she and Caldwell wrote together, did not measure up to *You Have Seen Their Faces.* She was often frustrated on the trip because Caldwell was very crabby and insecure. "My first

Fascism and Nazism: The Evils of State Control

Fascism was a form of government espoused by Benito Mussolini in Italy during the 1920s. Mussolini expected Italian citizens to obey the government's orders without question. In Germany, Adolf Hitler led the Nazi Party to power in 1933 and founded a government similar to Mussolini's. The Nazis believed they were part of an Aryan race that was superior to all other races. In order to rid Germany of the influences of other races, the Nazis established concentration camps that isolated Jews, non-Germans, homosexuals, communists, Romany, and other minority groups from the rest of the German population. Millions of people died in the concentration, and later, extermination camps.

thoughts," she remembered, "had to go toward Erksine and his moods, and my fondest hopes were that hidden glaciers would not come to the surface in the middle of an important series of pictures." Yet she was still considering marrying him, feeling that marriage might help Caldwell feel more secure.

In February of 1939, Bourke-White and Caldwell were married in a little church in Silver City, Nevada, but not before Caldwell signed a

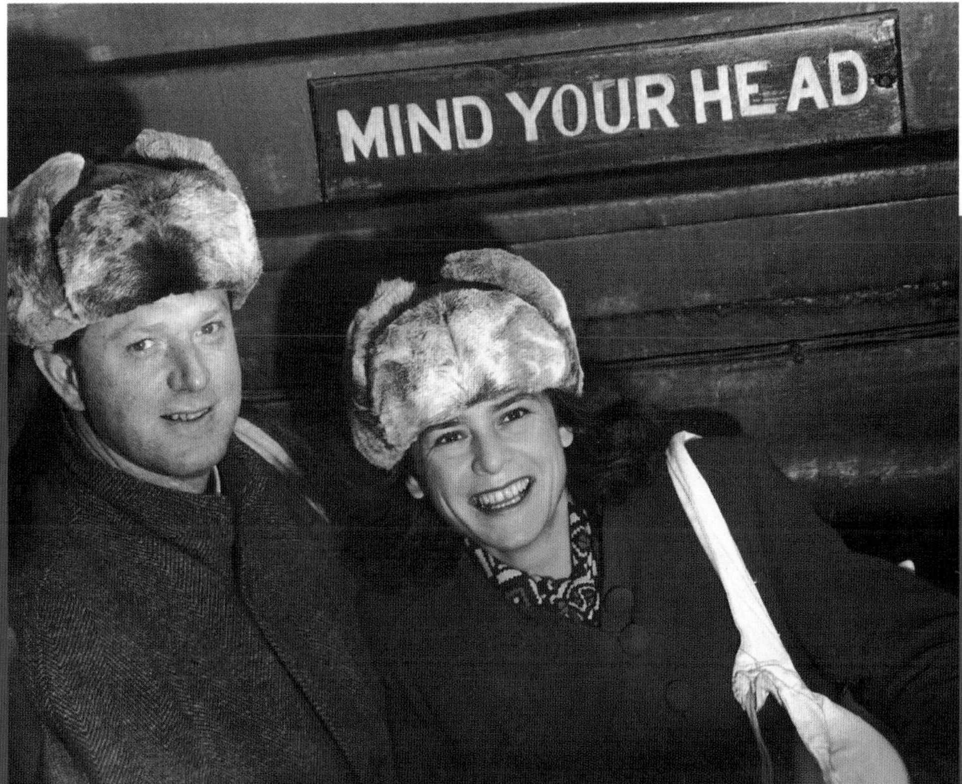

In the spring of 1941, Margaret Bourke-White and Erksine Caldwell began a journey that would take them all the way around the world. Here they are pictured on a ship taking them home from Europe in the fall of 1941.

marriage contract Bourke-White had written. In it, she asked Caldwell to be courteous toward her friends, to control his moods, and to try to work out whatever difficulties they were having before midnight. Lastly, she wrote, "There must be no attempts to snatch me away from photographic assignments." Caldwell agreed.

A NEW VENTURE

In the spring of 1940, Bourke-White left *Life* and joined *PM*, a new magazine headed by her former editor Ralph Ingersoll. She thought *PM* might better showcase her talents and offer her more opportunities for exhibiting her studies of insects and animals. *PM* was a revolutionary magazine in its design, content, and in the fact that it ran no advertising. However, it was not the right place for Bourke-White. She was used to being a star at *Fortune* and at *Life*, but *PM* was too busy establishing itself to give her the attention felt she deserved. After four months, she returned to *Life*.

SEVEN

Braving the Dangers

Bourke-White went to war before the rest of the United States did. In the spring of 1941, *Life* photo editor Wilson Hicks decided that she should go to the Soviet Union once again in order to cover the fragile peace that existed between the Germans and the Soviets. He sensed that the peace might not last, and he wanted a photographer there to cover the war, should it break out between the two nations. Germany had already invaded France and Poland, and World War II was threatening to consume every nation in Europe.

Bourke-White and Caldwell made their way to Moscow by going west through Asia, as traveling through Europe was too risky. They arrived in Moscow around the time of the White Nights, when the sun sets very late in the evening, and the sky stays light twenty-four hours a day. One month after their arrival, Germany and Russia were at war.

German planes bombed Moscow night after night. Civilians were ordered to stay underground in Moscow's subways, but Bourke-White wanted to get pictures of the air raids to send back to *Life*. One evening, when Caldwell was making a radio broadcast to the United States, she climbed up to the roof of the U.S. embassy and waited for the bombs to start falling. Soldiers in the German planes were dropping flares that would explode over the sky, illuminating the targets they wanted to hit. The bright light made it possible for Bourke-White to capture the buildings and the path of the fire from the antiaircraft guns shooting up into the sky. All of a sudden, Bourke-White sensed that a bomb was coming her way, and she rushed through an open window back into the embassy and lay down, covering her camera. Seconds later she was surrounded by shattered glass. She picked herself up and spent the rest of the night in the embassy basement.

Photographing the air raids was a strange experience for Bourke-White. "The sky is so startlingly big," she later wrote, "with its probing

While bombs fell nearby, Bourke-White kept taking pictures. This photograph shows the glow from the flares German planes used to illuminate Moscow, the flash from the bombs they were dropping on the city, and the fire from the Soviet anti-aircraft guns.

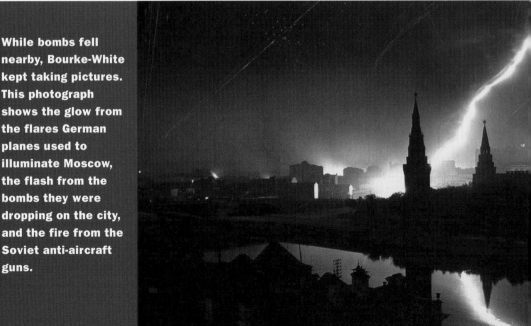

spears of searchlights and lines of fire, that man seems too small to count at all. In the first look at war, one feels immune; the spectacle is so strange, so remote, that it has no reality in terms of death and danger. But how quickly this feeling of immunity vanishes when one sees people killed!"

Bourke-White saw death firsthand when she traveled with the Soviet army to the front lines of the war. In her book *Shooting the Russian War*, she recounts how she and Caldwell were staying in the same hotel as officers of the Soviet air force. Early in the morning the Germans tried to bomb the hotel but missed and hit a home across the street. The only way Bourke-White was able to photograph the crumpled bodies of the dead inside was to treat the picture as "an abstract camera composition." Her focus on the technical issues became a sort of an emotional shield. If she thought about what lens to use or how long to keep the camera's shutter open, she could block out the overwhelming emotions that seeing death caused. However, once she had developed the negatives, she could not bring herself to look at them. The pain was too great.

Why would Bourke-White want to take a picture she didn't have the stomach to look at? Did she imagine others would be able to tolerate them? This is unlikely. She took pictures of whatever events occurred because recording them would help people learn the truth about the event. It takes less than a second to look at a picture of someone who was killed in a violent way and know that the death was terrible. We need not study the picture for hours in order to get its full effect. A glance is enough to make us flinch.

On the other hand, when we hear that a bomb has fallen on a house full of innocent civilians and has killed everyone inside, our imagination can do three things. It can try to picture what the death and destruction looks like. It can block the news by thinking of something else. Or it can save the news in our memory, and we can return to it later.

But when we look at a photograph, a reproduction of what actually happened enters our mind. Our minds are then stuck, if only for a moment, in trying to understand what our eyes have seen. While not everyone would agree that images have more power than sounds, in general, it is harder to forget the suffering we have seen than the suffering about which we have only heard. Bourke-White did not want the world to forget the horror of war. In notes for her autobiography, she expressed her desire to "build up the pictorial files of history" in order to make war seem less remote. The question of whether seeing the real effects of war discourages people from making war is still open. Nonetheless, as Bourke-White wrote in her notes, "Man has been failing long enough in his attempt to solve his problem by battles." Her pictures help remind us that "something more constructive is needed."

EMERGENCY AT SEA

Twenty-four hours after Bourke-White returned to the United States, she had to dash off on a lecture tour. Just before she was to speak at the University of Tennessee, the student chorus sang "America" (better known as "My Country 'Tis of Thee"). "I must have listened to the words, and sung them, hundred of times; but this time they sank into my mind," Bourke-White wrote in the last paragraph of *Shooting the Russian War*. "It seemed to me that never before had I actually heard the words of 'America,' and suddenly I found I was standing on the platform before all those university students—crying." She was relieved to be back home.

Bourke-White would not stay home for long. On December 7, 1941, Japanese planes attacked the U.S. naval base at Pearl Harbor. The United States, which up to this point had kept its troops out of the war, now felt it had to fight back. The air force accredited Bourke-White as its first official war photographer. Her pictures would be used by both *Life* and the Pentagon. Bourke-White was excited about this opportunity but was also very frustrated that she was not allowed to fly on a combat mission. She wanted to show people up close the risks air force pilots were taking, flying their planes over enemy territory where they could be shot down by an antiaircraft gun or enemy fighter plane. She had a lot of experience doing aerial photography and was confident that she could do an excellent job. But the men in charge thought combat flights were too dangerous for a woman. One experience was to change that.

War Brings Women New Roles

Because men were needed on the front lines of the war, women were asked to take over many of their jobs. Many of them served in the Women's Army Corps (WAC). While some women took over men's office duties, others were engaged near the front lines as nurses, cooks, drivers, mechanics, parachute riggers, and translators, and in many other functions. Other women took factory jobs, doing everything from working on assembly lines to operating forklifts. Some Americans were insecure about the idea of women doing jobs that had traditionally been done by men.

Late in 1942, Bourke-White sailed for North Africa with a group of ships ferrying soldiers and other personnel to the region. The journey along the coast of France, Spain, and Portugal, and through the Strait of Gibraltar was plagued by heavy storms. Sixty-foot (18 m) waves tossed the ships and sent dishes, furniture, and people tumbling. Everyone was relieved when they made it through the stormy Atlantic and entered the calm Mediterranean.

The calm sea provided a false comfort. Deep below, German submarines were waiting for the right time to torpedo the ships. When the moment came, most people on the ships were sleeping. A torpedo hit Bourke-White's ship deep below the surface of the water and made it lose its balance and lean heavily to one side. Bourke-White was thrown out of her bunk and onto the floor.

Rather than panic, Bourke-White began thinking calmly about what she should wear. By focusing on something practical, she was able to take her mind off the fact that her life was in danger. Once she had chosen which pair of pants and which coat to wear, she left her cabin and briefly joined the flow of people heading toward the lifeboats. Then she broke out of the line in order to head as quickly as she could to the ship's deck so she could take pictures. The moon was shining brightly, but there was not enough light for her to take photographs.

Nor was there much time. "Abandon ship!" the ship's loudspeaker rang out. The ship was sinking.

When Bourke-White made her way to the lifeboats, she noticed that her mouth was dry and sensed that the dryness was a sign of fear. When she was working, the physical dangers of the job did not scare her. All of her attention was on getting the best photograph possible. But now that her focus was on survival, she was more aware of how her body and mind were reacting to the emergency.

As she waited with the other passengers for their chance to get into a lifeboat and be lowered down to the sea, she had a realization. "We stood, all six thousand of us, at a crossroads, not just between personal death or life but between paralyzing self-concern and the thought for others that transcends self. We were in a situation too vast for any one person to control, a catastrophe where people will show the qualities they have."

Bourke-White was deeply impressed by the courage and sacrifice people around her were making. Some gave up their spots on the lifeboats and stayed on the ship in order to help their fellow passengers. Others were demonstrating their bravery by keeping their sense of humor. As Bourke-White remembers in her autobiography,

Bourke-White relishes her tea after being rescued from her torpedoed ship.

one nurse who had fallen into the water had started swimming alongside Bourke-White's lifeboat. "Which way to North Africa?" the nurse called out as she swam by.

Some of the soldiers who were sleeping on the bottom level of the ship lost their lives, but luckily most of the passengers escaped. They floated on the sea for most of the day until an English plane spotted them and called for a rescue ship.

THREATENING SKIES

Because she had already faced death, Jimmy Doolittle, the general in charge of the U.S. Air Force mission in North Africa, decided that there was no reason to be overprotective of her. Bourke-White got the go-ahead to fly in a bomber and was the first woman to have that distinction. She had a special flight suit of leather and thick wool designed for her, and the picture of her in the suit standing with camera in hand next to one of the B-17 fighter planes became a popular poster among the soldiers.

Her bombing mission took her over Tunisia, where the Germans had an airfield north of the city of Tunis. When the pilot was approaching the target, he made a series of maneuvers Bourke-White thought were in response to the commands she was giving to the pilot so that she could get the best angles for her photographs. The crew members on the flight were surprised to hear her voice. They had forgotten there was a woman on board.

Just as Bourke-White was looking down below at the damage the B-17's bombs had caused, she saw something coming toward her that she had to photograph. "In the air quite close to us were black spreading spiders, rather pretty, with legs that grew and grew. I couldn't imagine what they were, but again I dutifully photographed them, just in case." Then, all of a sudden, she realized that the spiders were in fact speeding masses of ammunition being fired at her plane by the Germans.

Luckily, the plane was only hit in the wing, and Bourke-White and the crew made it back to their base safely, as did thirty of the thirty-two planes that had set out on the mission. She later wrote, "Only after we were back . . . did I learn the bad news that two of the planes at the end of the formation that followed us had been shot down." Bourke-White seemed to accept the loss of these planes and of the men who flew them as an unavoidable part of war. She chose to focus her attention on the mission's successes, which distracted her from the loss. Back in New York, her editors published her photographs of the experience with the headline "*Life*'s Bourke-White Goes Bombing." With this title, they proved themselves to be as adept as she was at giving a dangerous mission a cheerful gloss.

Craters left from Allied bombing in the fields of Cassino in southern Italy made it difficult for the Germans to advance quickly over land.

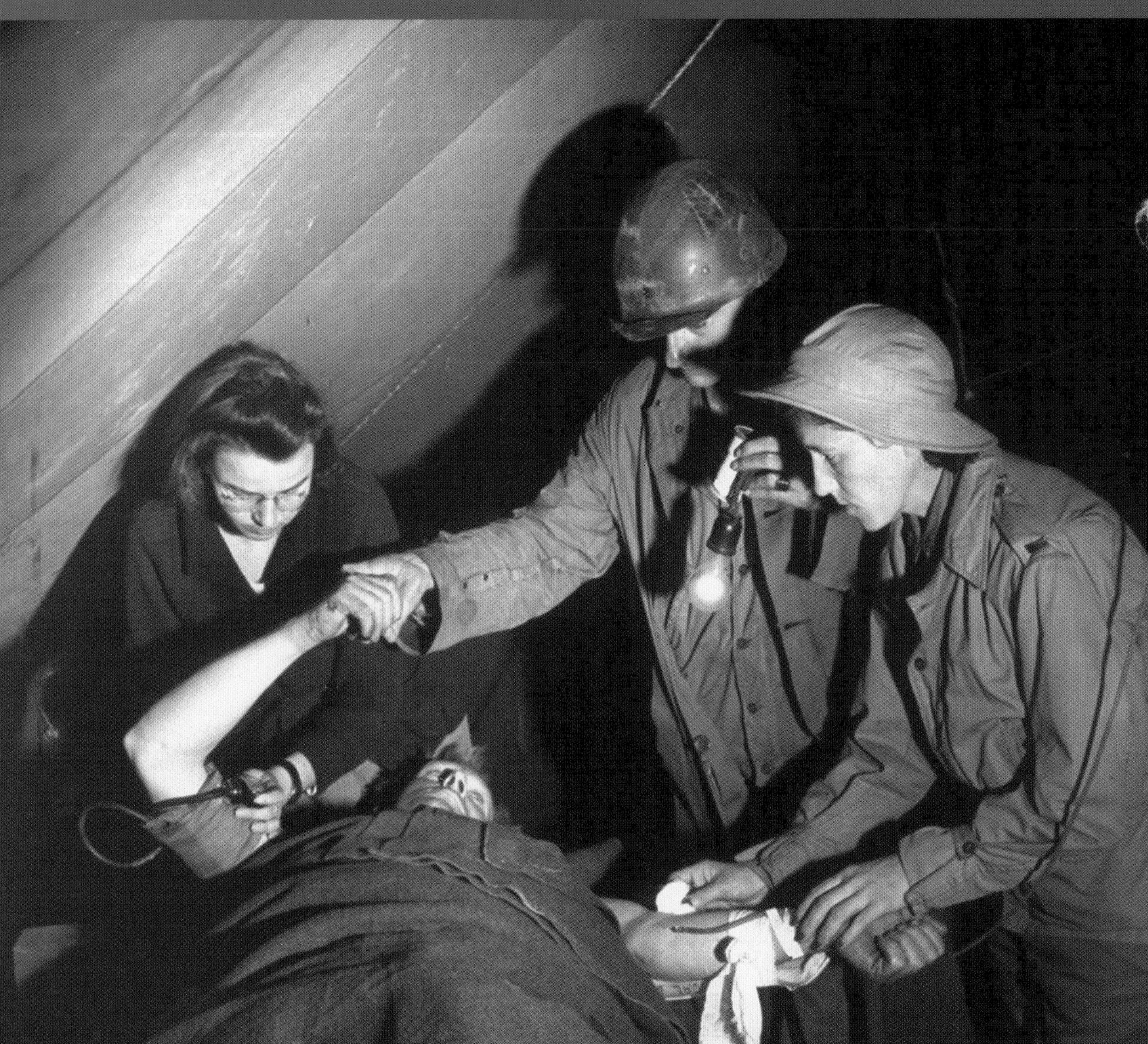

Bourke-White recorded the brave service of the female nurses who helped injured soldiers during World War II. A series of pictures Bourke-White shot of the nurses was lost by the Pentagon, and Margaret was never able to recover or publish them. Their loss pained her for the rest of her life.

EIGHT

Reasons to Fight

What can words do that photographs cannot? What can photographs do that words cannot? The books Bourke-White wrote about her experiences in Russia, Italy, and Germany during World War II help us think about these questions. Reading about physical violence can help us get a feeling of what war is really like, but seeing pictures of the injured or killed is a more powerful form of knowledge, because we react more quickly and more deeply to images. On the other hand, photographs of violence do not reveal the thinking behind those who caused or suffered from the violence. Only words can do that. By combining images and words in her three books about World War II, Bourke-White helped her readers understand both the physical and mental suffering of those it affected.

THE FORGOTTEN FRONT

Bourke-White had complained of the hours she spent making fake mud for the tire company advertising job, but she got more than her share of trekking through real mud while covering the Italian front. Toward the end of 1943, she asked *Life* to send her to Italy because she wanted to cover an area where the troops were in close fighting with the enemy. In North Africa she had only seen the enemy from the window of a fighter plane.

Corporal Jess Padgitt became her photo assistant, driving her over the muddy, mine-laden roads of Italy, where the Germans were fiercely defending a line across the northern part of the country. Other soldiers enthusiastically joined in helping Bourke-White get shots of the cannons they were firing, of the emergency surgeries field doctors and nurses were performing, or of the efforts of the engineering crews to build temporary pontoon (floating) bridges over the rivers the army needed to cross. Many of the soldiers had been fighting in Italy for months and were exhausted from the constant bombing by the enemy, which could happen at any time of the day, but was especially nerve-wracking when it happened in the middle of the night. They were excited to have Bourke-White there, recording their struggle for the Americans at home. Many of them felt like they had been forgotten, because other battles in France, Germany, and Asia captured more attention from the media, especially those conducted by daring fighter pilots.

Bourke-White wanted to give the readers of *Life* and *They Called It "Purple Heart Valley,"* her book about the Italian front, a sense of what was on the soldiers' minds. At one point, she relates a long conversation she had with a group of soldiers who had just completed building a bakery that was producing bread for the troops.

In *They Called It "Purple Heart Valley,"* Bourke-White writes of how she asked the soldiers what they thought life would be like when they returned home. One spoke about his hope that the government would help them get a college education, which he felt would prevent the widespread unemployment that had occurred when U.S. soldiers returned from World

Civil Rights Denied

While the United States had abolished slavery in 1865, many African Americans still struggled to enjoy the basic rights white Americans did. While their right to vote was granted to them by the Constitution through the passing of the Fifteenth Amendment in 1870, local laws in many states were enacted to prevent blacks from gaining political power. This was especially true in the South, where whites and blacks were segregated. In many establishments, blacks were not allowed to use the same facilities as whites were. Blacks could not attend the same schools as whites, nor did their schools receive as much funding from the federal or state government as the white-only schools did.

Many white Americans wanted the situation to stay the same. They were used to having more political and economic power than blacks did, and they were not willing to share. However, as Bourke-White noted, World War II had increased the nation's awareness that African Americans were brave defenders of their country. She hoped that in working together to defeat a common enemy, whites and blacks would get to know each other better and trust each other more.

War I. Another spoke in support of African American soldiers getting the right to vote as a reward for their military service. This caused some controversy in the group. A white soldier expressed the feeling that if blacks could vote, they might be able to win positions of power in society, which he felt they did not deserve. Responding to this, a soldier named Spike said, "It's quite a paradox . . . that we're fighting for democracy and yet the South is upset about the Negro vote." By exposing readers to the soldiers' conversations, Bourke-White was showing that they, like many Americans, were full of contradictions. They believed in fighting for democracy, but not all of them were sure everyone should be able to participate in it.

LOVE AND DEATH

Caldwell and Bourke-White had separated in the spring of 1942. He was not able to endure her long trips away from him, and she was not able to endure his grumpy moods. She was guarded about the split, but it must have affected her deeply to have failed a second time to make a marriage

Rewarding the Soldiers

In 1944, the United States enacted the G.I. Bill of Rights, which helped the soldiers returning from the war by paying for their educations, by offering them home loans at a low interest rate, and by giving them financial assistance if they could not find work. The veterans' organization, the American Legion, helped to make sure that the bill included African Americans and women.

work. In Italy she fell in love with Major Maxwell Jerome Papurt, whose nickname was Jerry. He was in charge of counterintelligence, leading spies who were secretly gathering information about the Germans. Papurt was not a handsome man, but Bourke-White loved his bright mind and his courage. She also relied on his encouragement. He knew she was afraid to try to love again, but he had faith in her. When she returned to the United States in the summer of 1944, she wrote to him every day, and he would write to her as often as he could. Then, in the fall of 1944, she heard news that he had been captured by the Germans.

Letters Papurt had sent to Bourke-White before his capture kept arriving. In a message to Papurt that the Vatican was broadcasting across enemy lines, Bourke-White said, "I love you. I will marry you." It is not known if he ever received the message. In late November the German hospital he was being held in was bombed by the Allies, and Papurt was killed. His letters to Bourke-White from earlier in the fall continued to arrive, even after his death. Imagine how heartbreaking it was for her to receive them.

Bourke-White returned to Italy in the fall of 1944 and then followed General George Patton into Germany in the spring of 1945, as the Germans were facing their end. One of the first places she visited was the concentration camp at Buchenwald, near the city of Weimar. What she saw there completely shocked her. "I saw and photographed the piles of naked, lifeless bodies, the human skeletons in furnaces, the living skeletons who would die the next day because they had to wait too long for deliverance, the pieces of tattooed skin for lampshades." As in the Soviet Union, focusing on getting a good photograph kept her from being overwhelmed by what she saw. "Buchenwald was more than the mind could grasp," she later wrote.

In *Dear Fatherland, Rest Quietly*, Bourke-White's book on post-war Germany, she writes of a Czech barber she met. He had been imprisoned in one of the concentration camps, and his story had moved her

The survivors of the Buchenwald concentration camp have the sunken faces of the starving, and the haunted eyes of the terrorized, and yet are full of hopeful energy. Bourke-White took this photograph soon after the camp was liberated.

deeply. Near the end of the war, the barber had heard news that the Nazis were going to kill all of his fellow prisoners. The Nazis knew the Americans were coming and did not want any of the prisoners to survive and see them defeated.

Late at night, the barber threw a rock into one of the rooms the other prisoners slept in, warning them about what was going to happen and telling them he would cut the wires in the electric fence surrounding the camp so they could escape without getting electrocuted. Most prisoners were too scared to follow his advice and soon met their death when the Nazis burnt down their mess hall while they were eating. Those who tried to escape the flames were shot.

When the barber returned to the camp after the Americans had come, Bourke-White saw him wandering around as if he was in search of something. At one point, he suddenly jumped down into a hole where some of the prisoners had been shot while trying to hide from the Nazis. He found a friend who had been murdered and looked around him for something he could take back as a memento for his friend's family. The only thing he could find was his countryman's false teeth. "For the wife of my friend," he said, placing them in his jacket.

LOOTING A WASTELAND

The defeat of Germany brought new responsibilities to the military forces of the countries that had crushed the German army. Bourke-White photographed the effect of the intense bombing from American and British warplanes, which had destroyed most of Germany's cities and factories. She photographed the Germans who had escaped from destruction or who had fled to avoid the bombing. They were returning to find their homes and businesses severely damaged or destroyed. Bourke-White recorded the Americans' response to the destruction and confusion with a very critical eye in her book.

Bourke-White was concerned that the United States was ignoring the opportunity to change the thinking of the people, especially the youth, whose minds had been poisoned by the teachings of the Nazis. They had been taught to hate their neighbors for their race, religion, political beliefs, or sexual orientation. Bourke-White believed that the United States was a place where most people were able to tolerate, and even respect, those with differing political and religious beliefs. She thought the United States was not doing enough to help shape education in Germany so that young Germans and Italians would become more understanding of political, religious, and racial differences.

With bitter irony, Bourke-White writes in *Dear Fatherland* of a conversation she had with a German woman who supported the Nazis'

Many of Germany's industrial centers looked like the city of Cologne after the Allied bombing. The Allies targeted these centers both in order to destroy the factories where weapons were made, and in order to crush the spirit of the German people. Over half a million civilians died in the bombing.

housing of minorities in concentration camps. Wasn't it similar to what existed in the American South, the German woman wondered aloud,

Devastation from the Sky

By the summer of 1945, the Allies had defeated the Germans, but the war in the Pacific still raged. At 8:15 A.M. on August 6, 1945, the U.S. B-26 bomber *Enola Gay* flew over the Japanese city of Hiroshima and dropped an atom bomb that exploded with a force the world had never before seen. Approximately eighty thousand people were killed instantly, and the city's buildings were flattened. Tens of thousands became chronically ill or died as a result of exposure to radiation from the explosion. The United States hoped that the death and destruction would cause the Japanese to surrender. When they did not, a few days later the Americans dropped another atom bomb, this time on the Japanese city of Nagasaki. The Japanese then surrendered, bringing an end to World War II.

Did America need to drop the atomic bomb in order to end the war, or would the Japanese have surrendered even without its use? Admiral William D. Leahy, Chief of Staff to Presidents Franklin Roosevelt and Harry Truman, wrote, "It is my opinion that the use of this barbarous weapon at Hiroshima and Nagasaki was of no material assistance in our war against Japan. The Japanese were already defeated and were ready to surrender because of the effective sea blockade and the successful bombing with conventional weapons." President Truman lacked this conviction. He chose to drop the bomb in what was at once an effort to protect American lives from the brutality of the Japanese Army, and a demonstration to the world of the technological and military supremacy of the United States.

where blacks and whites were segregated? The woman's question made Bourke-White think. To Bourke-White, it was unclear if the United States could teach Germans about tolerance and understanding when millions of blacks could not drink out of the same drinking fountains as whites, or dine in the same restaurants, or go to the same schools, or vote in the same elections.

American behavior regarding German property was a confusing matter for Bourke-White. A number of soldiers and other U.S. personnel were helping themselves to whatever they found in bombed-out or abandoned homes and businesses. To make this practice sound less criminal than stealing or looting, they called it "liberating." Bourke-White joined in the looting to a certain extent, trying to convince herself that she had some moral right to what she took. The German army, and the German citizens that had supported it, had robbed millions of people of their belongings and their lives. In her mind those who had risked their lives fighting against German aggression were entitled to German property, at least to a certain degree. But she did not think those who had come to Germany after the fighting should participate in the looting.

War is a very stressful environment that can make people act in ways they wouldn't normally. Bourke-White herself noted that looting had a "curious psychology." As she wrote, "For weeks, months or years that enemy has been shooting away at you. When you move into his hometown, you feel you own it. You're overwhelmingly curious to see how he lived and what kind of fellow he was. It becomes a fever, highly contagious."

In Bourke-White's mind the greatest injustice that arose from the looting was the development of the black market. In the black market, stolen goods were sold for prices that were much higher than normal. Sellers were also able to set high prices for goods that were hard to find or rationed. If someone wanted more butter than the government would allow one person to have during the forced economizing of wartime, for example, she could buy it on the black market for a higher price. Bourke-White did not think soldiers should be selling goods they had looted on the black market for inflated prices. When millions of people were hungry, and hundreds of thousands were homeless, profiting from their stolen goods seemed immoral.

Bourke-White's books on World War II gave readers the chance to understand the war in a more thorough way than *Life*'s shorter articles did. By writing books about her experiences, she avoided having to include the magazine advertisements that might have distracted readers from her report on the soldiers' bravery and confusion. She was able to write longer portrayals of individuals involved in the war, such as Alfried Krupp, a German industrialist who had used the people being held in concentration camps as slave laborers, but who denied that anything wrong or immoral had taken place. Her chapters in *Dear Fatherland* relating her conversations with him were later used at his trial for war crimes as evidence against him.

NINE

The Price of Division

In 1946, *Life* asked Bourke-White to go to India to cover its fight for independence. The British had ruled India for almost ninety years, but the Indians had been struggling for their freedom for much of that time. Under the leadership of Mohandas Gandhi, Indians were making advances toward ending British rule. Gandhi's campaigns of nonviolent demonstrations and boycotts were slowly putting more power into the hands of the Indians. Gandhi felt that Indians would have greater moral authority and gain more sympathy for their cause if they attempted to end British rule without using violence. Even if the British attacked Indians, he felt they should not strike back.

Much of Gandhi's work to end British rule had already been accomplished by the time Bourke-White went to India. People admired the way Gandhi had politely yet firmly stood up to the British, breaking their laws when he found them unjust and leading many others to do so. One of his most famous acts of civil disobedience was the Salt March in which he led Indians to the sea to harvest their own salt in protest of the British salt tax, which had been a great burden on many Indians. When Bourke-White went to Gandhi's headquarters for an interview and to take his portrait, she knew she was going to be in the presence of one of the world's most respected men, but she failed to show it. Instead, she assumed that Gandhi's secretary would be impressed by her credentials as a famous *Life* photojournalist with a very important assignment to do.

It was fitting that Bourke-White's sometimes egotistical nature should be tested in India, a land where many strive to control their pride through spiritual practice. By the age of forty-two, Bourke-White had achieved so much in her life that she could be excused for thinking highly of herself. She had certainly shown that she was able to make every sacrifice to excel at what she did, and could argue that the world was enriched by her efforts. Nevertheless, Bourke-White's concern with broadcasting the worth of her own achievements was not her most attractive quality, and it distanced people from her.

Gandhi's secretary interpreted her attitude as a sign that she was not ready to meet with Gandhi. In order for her to approach Gandhi with the right understanding, he told her that she must learn to spin cloth using the *charka*, the spinning wheel that Gandhi used. At first Bourke-White objected, saying that she did not have time. But when she saw that the secretary was serious, she decided to learn. She knew that Gandhi thought of the charka as a symbol of India's independence, as it was a native Indian tool the Indians had relied on for thousands of years to weave their cloth. The British had used economic means and physical violence to discourage Indians from using the charka in order to destroy India's textile industry. For Gandhi, making cloth with the charka was another sign of resistance.

Once Bourke-White had learned to spin, Gandhi met with her. However, it was Gandhi's day of silence, so she was only able to take his portrait. Her photograph of Gandhi sitting at his spinning wheel became one of Bourke-White's best-known images, as it captured Gandhi's calm focus and spiritual presence.

Bourke-White traveled all over India with the Indian photographer Sunil Janah, documenting many of the trials Indians were going through, including famine, poverty, and class discrimination. She visited a tannery, where children were forced to work in vats of dangerous chemicals curing leather. She spoke to tenant farmers whose living and working conditions were similar to those of tenant farmers living in the American South. And she photographed the powerful and wealthy of India, some of whom lived in mansions as lavish as any Westerner had ever seen.

Mohandas Gandhi was one of India's greatest political and spiritual leaders. He also inspired political leaders around the world, including the Reverend Martin Luther King, Jr. Bourke-White's image of Gandhi at his spinning wheel is one of her most famous.

Bourke-White saw both the extreme wealth as well as the extreme poverty that existed in India. In this picture, a money lender is conversing with his two sons.

A New Generation of Nations

India's fight to rid itself of the British occupation was one of many similar fights around the world in which natives led both nonviolent and violent movements for self-determination and control of their resources. The Philippines gained independence from the United States in 1946, Indonesia from Holland in 1949, and Algeria, after a long war, gained independence from France in 1962. By the mid-1970s, more than sixty nations had come into being that had not existed at the beginning of the century.

One of the hardest experiences Bourke-White had was photographing those who had died in the Calcutta riots of August 1946. Thousands of dead bodies lay on Calcutta's streets, reminding Bourke-White of the horrors she had seen at Buchenwald. The riot had resulted from the conflict between Muslims and Hindus over the need many Muslims felt to have their own country. They felt that when India achieved independence, the Hindu majority would elect a government comprised mainly of Hindus, and Muslims would not be safe or have equal rights. In addition, some Muslims wanted to live in a country that more closely followed Islamic law.

GANDHI'S LAST DAYS

In January of 1948, more riots broke out in India. By this point, India had won independence from the British and had separated into two countries. Unconnected sections of the northwest and northeast of India became Pakistan. Millions of Hindus left the newly created Pakistan, and millions of Muslims left India in the largest migration the world had ever known. During the migration, much violence occurred. In order to calm the tension and create peace between the Muslims and Hindus, the seventy-eight-year-old Gandhi decided to fast, as he had done many times before. During his fasts he would stop eating and drinking in order to bring attention to the suffering of others. As people saw Gandhi losing physical strength over the course of his fasts, some of which lasted for a week or more, they would seek to find solutions to their problems.

Bourke-White was very impressed to see Gandhi risking his life to help others. She saw how thousands of people would gather in support of Gandhi. After six days of fasting, Gandhi received a number of telegrams from Hindu and Muslim religious leaders promising to work for peace, and he ended his fast. "It was a moving experience," Bourke-White remembered later, "to be there and see the people laughing and crying for joy."

A few days later, Bourke-White was leaving India and went to say good-bye to Gandhi. She told him of the book she was writing on India and asked him for answers to many questions her experience in India had raised. While Bourke-White admired Gandhi as a spiritual leader, she had a hard time understanding Gandhi's position on industry. She wanted to know if Gandhi was really against machines, which had revolutionized life in the West. For Bourke-White the machine "cares nothing about a man's ancestors; it does not feel polluted by his touch, knows no prejudice." Bourke-White felt that factories would bring different people together and involve them in a new way of working. But for Gandhi, the machine was not the solution for India's problems. He felt that it took

Muslims and Hindus were not the only religious groups that migrated in large numbers once India was divided into India and Pakistan. Here, Sikhs make their way to the Punjab region in northwestern India.

jobs away from people by making automatic many processes that were once done by hand. And he felt that many things the machine produced were not really necessary. His focus was on changing people's hearts, and he felt material things distracted people from trying to do good.

A few hours after Bourke-White left Gandhi, he was shot and murdered by a Hindu fanatic. Bourke-White rushed back to try to take a picture of Gandhi, but was blocked by his family and supporters. Later, she photographed the crowds that had gathered for his cremation, and climbed on top of a truck to take pictures of the fire that was turning Gandhi's body to ashes.

Bourke-White's need to get a picture of whatever she considered newsworthy raises a number of questions. When is it wrong to take a picture? When someone's family does not want you to, as was the case with Gandhi's family after he had been shot? When you wouldn't want someone to take a picture of you in the same condition? Any time you have not asked for permission?

Many photojournalists struggle with these questions. They sometimes feel pressure to get an image that will shock their audience, and they must compete with reporters from rival publications to shoot the most powerful pictures. Invading peoples' privacy may become routine, or even exciting to reporters. Furthermore, when their papers show the world what people are truly doing, these pictures can have a lot of power. Photographs can be used in a court of law to convict someone of a crime. If someone is committing a criminal act, should the photographer ask permission of the criminal before taking the picture?

Regarding Bourke-White's behavior, there were certainly times in her long career as a photojournalist that she invaded people's privacy and made people furious in doing so. She could certainly be insensitive, as she was towards Gandhi's family after his murder. They were stricken with grief and needed peace, not the anxious energy of a prying photographer. In general, however, many believe that history is better served by the photojournalist who risks upsetting people. Events do not pause until a photographer has permission to record them. In the end, a photojournalist's primary devotion must be to shooting images powerful enough to capture the essence of important stories. Bourke-White repeatedly proved she had this devotion. When we look at her photographs, we understand why she took the risks she did.

FINDING A CONTACT

Bourke-White felt that her experiences in India were the most important in her life, in particular witnessing Gandhi's devotion to his people. After she finished *Halfway to Freedom*, her book on India, *Life* asked Bourke-White to cover South Africa, a country famous for its diamond and gold mines. Bourke-White would again come head to head with abusive labor practices and racism. In South Africa, as Bourke-White would point out, 2.5 million whites ruled more than 8.5 million blacks. She could not see the justice in that.

At first Bourke-White had trouble making contacts with the black South Africans she wanted to photograph. Part of the problem was that black South Africans were controlled by a system called apartheid, which translates to "apartness." The laws of apartheid were designed to keep black south Africans segregated from whites, as well as to restrict their access to education, health care, and political and legal representation.

Yet one day, while walking by the water in Cape Town, a city near the tip of South Africa, she heard a voice calling. As Bourke-White recalls in her autobiography, a black woman approached her and pulled out a copy of *You Have Seen Their Faces*, one that was worn from having been read many times. Bourke-White now had her contact, someone who knew Bourke-White's work and could tell other black South Africans that Bourke-White would do a good job of capturing their story.

In gold and diamond mines that were over a mile under the earth, black South Africans worked in conditions little better than slavery.

DIAMONDS, GOLD, AND GRAPES

Many of the black South African men whom Bourke-White photographed could not read. They signed job contracts for mining jobs with their thumbprints after having heard them read out loud. Visiting the men's dormitory at the mine where men were doing traditional dances to keep their spirits up, she became fascinated by two dancers and ventured to ask their names. She found that they were not known by their names, but only by the numbers that had been assigned to them when they applied to work at the mine. She decided she wanted to do a series of photographs of them in the mine, but when she asked where they worked, she was told that it was in a very dangerous area where the earthen roof sometimes caved in on the miners, who would become trapped below. The mine manager suggested that he show her a different part of the mine.

Whatever fear she felt at the time likely vanished when Bourke-White sensed he was saying no to her idea. Here was another mystery to uncover. She insisted on going. She descended in a human-size bucket through a narrow shaft, down to a mine passageway 2 miles (3.2 km) below the surface of the earth. Crawling through the tight, damp passageways of the mine, she came across the two dancers she had seen in the dormitory. In one of her most famous photographs, she captured the punishing exhaustion on their faces as sweat dripped down their torsos. Bourke-White was struck by the difference between their lives above and below ground.

Soon after taking the photograph, Bourke-White had to be evacuated from the mine. The heat and poor air circulation had made her throat so tight she could not even swallow the water a mine supervisor had given her. Heading up to the surface, she realized how lucky she was to be able to escape the mine as soon as someone felt that her health depended on it. The mine workers, on the other hand, would have to spend eight hours in the suffocating mine, and then wait for hours more as the mine elevators took the white supervisors up to the surface first.

Mining was not the only industry in which whites were abusing black South Africans. Bourke-White visited a vineyard where children had been hired to pick grapes. Part of their pay was given to them in wine. At five o'clock in the morning, they would be given one serving of wine called a tot. Throughout the day they would receive four more tots. Paying the children in wine served three purposes. It saved the vineyard owners money, it made the children dependent on alcohol, and it created future customers, namely the children who would buy the wine when they grew up. The system disgusted and angered Bourke-White, especially because she could not see how the situation for the children would ever improve while apartheid existed, as black children had few rights.

In her pictures for *Life*, Bourke-White made sure to capture not only the miserable conditions of the black South Africans but also the beautiful surroundings in which the natives were abused. *Life*'s viewers could then see that South Africa's geography, with its lush fields and dramatic seaside cliffs, was a kind of dream world, but that its society was a nightmare.

A Man of Great Patience

One of the leaders of the black South Africans in their struggle against apartheid was Nelson Mandela. At first Mandela was a follower of Gandhi's principle of nonviolent protest, but when white South African police officers shot and killed sixty-nine unarmed protesters in a demonstration in Sharpeville in 1960, Mandela began to call for armed resistance to apartheid. Largely because of his support of armed struggle, he was sent to jail for life in 1964 but was released in 1990, just as President F. W. de Klerk was ending apartheid. Mandela became the first black president of South Africa in 1994.

The roaring jet power of the B-36 bomber can be felt in this photograph Bourke-White shot at the Carswell Strategic Air Command base in Fort Worth, Texas, in 1951.

TEN

A Will of Steel

In the years since the end of World War II, the United States had grown very concerned that the Soviets might try to attack with nuclear weapons in an attempt to spread communism all over the world. The U.S. military built bombers that could travel all the way to the Soviet Union at nearly the speed of sound, drop bombs on the Soviet's military installations, and then return to the United States without landing to refuel. They hoped that if the Soviets knew they had bombers this powerful, the Soviets would think twice about firing a nuclear missile at the United States. In the winter of 1951, about a year after she had returned from South Africa, Bourke-White had a new adventure in the skies. She was assigned to photograph the planes and the crew of the Strategic Air Command, the section of the U.S. military that would respond to a nuclear attack.

Bourke-White became one of the first women to fly in the bombers. She photographed one of them being refueled in midair and photographed the huge bomb bay from which the nuclear bombs would be dropped. One of the planes took Bourke-White 41,000 feet (12,496.8 m) into the air. "The sky was a color such as I've never seen," she wrote in her *Life* photo-essay, "the darkest blue imaginable, yet luminous like the hottest cobalt, too brilliant for the eyes to bear." *Life* hoped that Bourke-White's photo-essay would help convince the American public, more than twenty million of whom read *Life* every week, that the military had the power to protect it.

Not everyone was reassured by Bourke-White's article covering the Strategic Air Command. The journalist Westbrook Pegler accused Bourke-White of sympathizing with communists and questioned how she was allowed access to the one of the United States' main defenses against the Soviets. In one of his newspaper columns, Pegler wrote that Bourke-White had been cited thirteen times for ties to communism by

Competing in the Heavens

In the late 1950s, Bourke-White was given permission to be *Life*'s first photojournalist in outer space, should the opportunity arise. Her request came during the what was called the "space race" between the Soviet Union and the United States. The Soviets took the lead early by launching the first satellite and putting the first living being in space (the dog Laika). In 1969, the United States caught up with the Soviets by landing a manned spacecraft on the moon.

the House Un-American Activities Committee (HUAC), a congressional body in charge of investigating Americans with suspected communist links. Pegler's attack was a little suspicious as Hearst, the news corporation that published his articles, was very competitive with the Time-Life Corporation that published Bourke-White's work. Pegler's attempt to link Time-Life's founder, Henry Luce, to the negative publicity he was heaping on Bourke-White suggests that his concern about Bourke-White's communist sympathies was a charade.

The situation was no game for Bourke-White, however. Pegler's columns had stirred the HUAC to focus greater attention on Bourke-White. The HUAC had noted that Bourke-White had her name on the board of certain organziations that were accused of being sympathetic to communism or to be covers for communist activity. Bourke-White's involvement with the American Artists' Congress was one of the concerns of the committee. In a 1936 speech to the American Artists' Congress, she had praised the freedom available to Soviet artists.

Other information the HUAC felt was damaging came from Bourke-White's FBI file. The FBI had been spying on Bourke-White since 1940 in order to discover whether her ties to communism endangered the United States. But while one part of government was suspicious of Bourke-White, another part had her full confidence: the U.S. military. In fact, she had been given a citation by the air force for her work as a war correspondent.

Bourke-White was shocked and saddened by the accusations of Pegler and the HUAC, and she had reason to be worried as well. Her career could be ruined by the accusations, as people might refuse to work with her. She could be thrown in jail. She could be executed for being a spy.

In a statement written for the committee, Bourke-White explained that she was not, nor had she ever been a member of the Communist Party, and that she believed in democracy. She also reminded the committee that in World War II she had served her country with great devotion. While this was enough to satisfy the HUAC, Bourke-White was still nervous about her reputation.

A Climate of Fear

In the late 1940s and early 1950s, a climate of fear existed in the United States, in no small part because of the work of Republican senator Joseph McCarthy of Wisconsin. Senator McCarthy teamed up with J. Edgar Hoover, director of the FBI, to fight what was called "the Red Scare." Americans were told that communists were threatening U.S. security, and that action must be taken to expose and defeat the menace. As chairman of the government Committee on Operations of the Senate, McCarthy had the authority to call citizens before Congress and ask them to name people they thought were linked to communism. Some of the most famous Americans of the day faced the committee, including a large contingent of Hollywood actors, screenwriters, and producers. While some chose to help McCarthy with his witch hunt, others did not. As a result they were blacklisted, which meant they were not allowed to work in Hollywood.

Losing one's livelihood was not the only consequence of being singled out as a communist. On June 19, 1953, Julius and Ethel Rosenberg were executed by the U.S. government. They were charged with spying for the Soviet Union and helping it acquire the knowledge of how to build an atomic bomb.

A DIFFERENT ANGLE

Bourke-White decided that she would go to Korea and cover the war that was raging there. The republican South Korea, supported by the U.S. army, was fighting against the communists who controlled the north of the country. By covering South Korea's battle against the communists, Bourke-White hoped that her patriotism would no longer be questioned. She wanted to focus on a side of the war she did not feel other journalists had—that of the effect of the war on the communities and families from which its fighters came.

Bourke-White found the situation in Korea heartbreaking. Many families had brothers who were fighting on opposite sides of the war. Villages were divided, and mothers and fathers of the fighters were in great emotional pain. South Korea had begun a tactic of broadcasting recordings of songs and the voices of village elders into the mountains, where the many of communists were based, hoping that fighters in the hills would hear them, feel homesick, and return.

One fighter who abandoned the communists after spending two years with them was a man named Nim Churl-Jin. Bourke-White decided to follow Churl-Jin as he returned to his family's village. She photographed his reunion with his wife and child and his tense encounter with his older brother, who was very angry with Churl-Jin for joining the communist rebels. As night began to fall, word came that Churl-Jin's mother, who thought that he was dead, was on her way back from another village with her relatives. Bourke-White raced with Churl-Jin to find his mother, hoping to catch her before the light was lost. "In a whole lifetime of taking pictures," Bourke-White wrote later in her autobiography, "a photographer knows that the time will come when he will take one picture that seems the most important of all." For Bourke-White, the moment had come. Churl-Jin's mother was approaching on a path across a brook. Churl-Jin dashed across the brook, with Bourke-White and her tiny 35 mm camera close behind. Taking his mother in his arms, he assured her against her protestations that it was really him. He wasn't dead. Finally she believed him, and as they sank down in the grass, she began singing him a lullaby.

Bourke-White's picture of Churl-Jin being embraced by his mother captures some of their immense joy in being reunited. However, it is more important as a record of what Bourke-White thought was her best example of capturing a relatively spontaneous moment.

Once she had been fascinated with machines and with the bright lights and bulky cameras that helped to reveal their beauty. By the time she photographed Churl-Jin and his mother, her foremost need was to capture human drama with the simplest photographic means.

Love and shame are intermixed in Bourke-White's photograph of Nim Churl-Jin's reunion with his mother.

THE GREATEST BATTLE

Much of Bourke-White's life was spent either abroad or in New York City, but Connecticut was where she went to escape. Her house in Darien was about an hour north of New York City. Deep in the woods, it was a relaxing place where she could think and write. In her autobiography, Bourke-White writes of how she loved to sleep outside with her cat guarding her. As soon as the dawn would come, he would know his watch was over, and would curl up next to Bourke-White and sleep.

Bourke-White liked to wake up early and write. She felt very fresh in the morning. In the quiet, there was nothing to distract her, and the voices and sights of her travels would come back to her uninterrupted. But when Bourke-White began working on her autobiography in the mid-1950s, she found that something was keeping her from writing. Her arms and fingers would become too stiff for her to

Under the watchful eye her beloved cat Sita, Bourke-White plays catch while walking near her home in Darien, Connecticut. Margaret's physical therapy helped her to retrain her body, which had lost much of its agility due to the effects of Parkinson's disease.

operate her typewriter. After sitting for a long time, she would have trouble getting back up.

She was puzzled. "I had always been arrogantly proud of my health and durability," she later remembered. "Strong men might fall by the wayside, but I was 'Maggie the Indestructible.'" Her pride was quickly set aside, however, so that she could regain the flexibility she needed to write her autobiography and keep working as a photojournalist. Soon she was following a strict schedule of physical therapy, taking long walks to keep her legs limber, and twisting wet towels to keep her arms loose.

At first Bourke-White tried to hide her illness from her friends, but eventually she was able to tell them that she had been diagnosed with Parkinson's disease. She was upset with herself for not telling them sooner, because they had wanted to support her but did not know how without

A Mysterious Malady

Parkinson's disease results from a lack of cells that produce dopamine, a chemical responsible for communicating movement commands in the brain. When dopamine production falls, the brain loses its power to regulate movement. Sufferers of Parkinson's can have difficulty controlling their limbs and can experience trouble talking, walking, and maintaining their balance. The causes of Parkinson's disease are not known, although genetic factors and exposure to toxins and metals have been suggested as possibilities.

The actor Michael J. Fox has Parkinson's disease and has done much to promote research for a cure. His foundation's Web site can be found at michaeljfox.org.

acknowledging what she was trying to keep secret. In Bourke-White's view, Parkinson's disease "works its way into all paths of life, into all that is graceful and human and outgiving in our lives, and poisons it all."

Bourke-White had two very controversial brain surgeries in order to try and reduce the effects of Parkinson's. These had mixed results. Flexibility returned to her limbs, but her speech was affected. In spite of the great physical burden that had been placed on her, Bourke-White continued to write her autobiography, which was published to much acclaim in 1963.

LEAVING A LEGACY

Bourke-White's brave battle against Parkinson's disease impressed many people. Americans learned of her struggle in a television play broadcast in the early 1960s and in a *Life* photo-essay shot by her longtime friend, the photographer Alfred Eisenstaedt. Visitors to Bourke-White's house in Darien were amazed by her passion for life. As Sean Callahan, then a young photo editor, remembers, "The most compelling feature was her blue-grey eyes, bright and clear and penetratingly sharp. . . . I soon realized that her eyes were not affected by the paralysis, and, whether consciously or not, this was how she animated her side of a conversation. Her eyes literally danced, and she used them to replace gesture, tone, and posture."

In late August of 1971, Bourke-White fell down the stairs of her house in Darien and was taken to the hospital with a broken rib. On August 27, she died. Until the end, she had insisted on living at home despite her debilitating illness with which she had battled for almost two decades.

In Bourke-White's sixty-seven years of life, she had followed her dreams with a will of steel. As Bourke-White herself said, she had to use her camera as a mirror, a net, and a sieve, all in order to help people reflect on life. The legacy she left for us is in her images and words. They burn with her passion to uncover the truth and the beauty of the world in which we live.

Today's Women Photojournalists

In Bourke-White's day there were few women photojournalists. In today's world there are many women covering important events all over the world and sending back their digital photographs by satellite. Studies show that women in journalism are paid, on average, a lower salary than are men. Furthermore, many women in journalism find that men's macho attitudes still persist in the newsroom, as does sexual harassment. But although women may still have to struggle with sexism, they have certain advantages men do not have. For example, Kate Brooks, a photojournalist who has worked in Afghanistan and Iraq, has pointed out that women photojournalists can go into female-only areas, such as those in the Muslim world, and thus better document women's experiences.

Timeline

MARGARET BOURKE-WHITE'S LIFE   WORLD EVENTS

1904 Margaret Bourke-White is born to Joseph White and Minnie Bourke on June 14 in New York City.

1914 World War I begins.

1918 World War I ends.

1920 Women gain the right to vote.

1921 In the spring Margaret graduates from Plainfield High School. In the fall she begins the first of two semesters at Columbia University in New York City.

1922 Margaret's father dies. In the spring she studies photography and design with the influential professor Clarence H. White. In the fall she attends the University of Michigan on a full scholarship.

1923 Time magazine publishes its first issue.

1924 Margaret marries Everett Chapman on June 13 in Michigan. They move to Indiana, where Everett teaches and Margaret begins her fourth year of college, both at Purdue University.

1925 Margaret moves to Cleveland, Ohio, where she takes classes at Case Western Reserve University.

1926 Margaret, having separated from Everett, transfers to Cornell University, where she continues her studies. There, Margaret photographs and sells pictures of the campus's buildings and environs.

1927 After graduation Margaret returns to Cleveland and officially divorces Everett. She begins work as an architectural photographer and sells her first commercial photograph.

1928 In Germany Dr. Erich Salomon's series of candid photographs of newsworthy affairs help to establish photojournalism.

1929 Margaret's photographs of the Otis Steel mills are reproduced in *Nation's Business* magazine. Later in the year she begins her first assignment for *Fortune* magazine.

The stock market crashes, resulting in a worldwide economic depression.

1930 She moves her studio from Cleveland to the sixty-first floor of the newly completed Chrysler Building in New York City. Margaret visits the USSR and becomes the first foreign photographer permitted to take pictures of Soviet industry.

Germany introduces the Leica Camera, a small 35 mm, 36-exposure camera.

1931 Margaret publishes her first book, *Eyes on Russia*. Later that year she returns to the USSR on an invitation from the Soviet government.

1932 Amelia Earhart becomes the first woman to fly solo across the Atlantic Ocean.

1933 Franklin Delano Roosevelt is elected president of the United States. The first concentration camp is established in southern Germany.

Margaret is awarded commissions for two separate photographic murals in New York City, one for the National Broadcasting Company and the other for the Consulate of the Soviet Union.

1934 The Midwest suffers from the worst drought in U.S. history.

Margaret documents the drought's devastating effects on the population.

1936 The first multilayered color film, Kodachrome, is developed.

Margaret travels through the American South with Erskine Caldwell for their book on sharecropping and tenant farming. In the fall, her photo of the Fort Peck Dam is chosen for the cover of the first issue of *Life* magazine.

1937 The book Margaret wrote with Erskine, *You Have Seen Their Faces*, is published.

1938 Margaret travels with Erskine to Czechoslovakia and Hungary in preparation for writing her second book.

1939 World War II begins.

1939–1940 Margaret marries Erskine Caldwell. She journeys to Romania, Turkey, Syria, Egypt, and England on an assignment for *Life*.

1940 The FBI groups Margaret with thousands of other Americans suspected of sympathizing with the Communist Party.

Margaret travels with Erskine across the United States, taking photographs for their book *Say, Is This the USA?*

1941 Margaret journeys through China into the USSR and is the only American photographer in Moscow when Germany attacks.

The Japanese bomb Pearl Harbor on December 7.

1942 Margaret writes *Shooting the Russian War*. Margaret and Erskine divorce. Traveling from England to North Africa aboard a military convoy, Margaret survives a German torpedo attack.

1943 Margaret is the first woman to travel in a B-17 and document an air force bombing raid.

1943–1944 Margaret covers the Italian front for *Life* and for her book *They Called It "Purple Heart Valley."*

1945 Hitler commits suicide. The United States drops atomic bombs on Hiroshima and Nagasaki, killing hundreds of thousands of civilians. World War II ends.

Margaret photographs Germany as its concentration camps are liberated and its cities and industrial centers are seized by American, Russian, and British forces.

1946 Margaret covers India for *Life*.

1947 India wins independence from the United Kingdom.

The Polaroid camera is invented.

1948 Margaret travels to India for the second time and interviews Gandhi hours before his assassination.

1949 China becomes the People's Republic of China, a communist nation. The Cold War begins as the Soviet Union detonates its first atomic device.

1949 Margaret travels to South Africa and photographs the effects of apartheid on black South Africans.

1950 The Korean War begins as the communist North battles the anticommunist South. Senator Joseph McCarthy leads a committee investigating Americans for suspected communist sympathies.

1951 Margaret's name comes before McCarthy's committee as a suspected communist sympathizer due to the efforts of the journalist Westbrook Pegler.

1952 Margaret travels to Japan to cover the U.S. occupation and then to Korea to photograph civilians and soldiers during the Korean War.

1953 Stalin dies.

1955 Margaret's photographs are included in "The Family Man" exhibit at the Museum of Modern Art, an exhibit that will travel to more than thirty countries and be seen by nearly nine million people.

1957 *Sputnik*, an unmanned satellite, is launched from the Soviet Union.

1957 *Life* publishes Margaret's last story, as Parkinson's disease prevents her from continuing to work as a photojournalist.

1959 Margaret undergoes the first of two brain surgeries to curb the progression of Parkinson's disease.

1963 Margaret publishes her autobiography, *Portrait of Myself*.

The Reverend Martin Luther King, Jr., a civil rights leader inspired by Gandhi, gives his "I Have a Dream" speech on the steps of the Lincoln Memorial in Washington, D.C., on August 28.

President John F. Kennedy is assassinated in Dallas on November 22.

1964 The Civil Rights Act is signed by President Lyndon B. Johnson.

1968 Martin Luther King, Jr. is assassinated in Memphis on April 4.

1969 American astronauts land on the moon on July 20.

1971 Margaret dies on August 27 in Darien, Connecticut.

To Find Out More

BOOKS

Bourke-White, Margaret, and Sean Callahan, Maryann Kornely, Debra Cohen, eds. *Margaret Bourke-White: Photographer.* New York: Bulfinch, 1998.

Bourke-White, Margaret and Erskine Caldwell. *You Have Seen Their Faces.* Athens: University of Georgia Press, 1995.

Colman, Penny. *Where the Action Was: Women War Correspondents in World War II.* New York: Crown Books for Young Readers, 2002.

Phillips, Stephen Bennett. *Margaret Bourke-White: The Photography of Design, 1927–1936.* New York: Rizzoli, 2003.

ORGANIZATIONS AND ONLINE SITES

Foto8
http://foto8.com/search/index.html

This site offers visitors a chance to view photographic essays from all over the world.

Newseum
http://www.newseum.org/cybernewseum/

This is a cybermuseum with exhibits, activities, and games relating to journalism.

Special Collections Research Center, Syracuse University Library
http://libwww.syr.edu/digital/guides/m/MargaretBourkeWhitePapers-Inv.htm

The Special Collections Research Center holds the Margaret Bourke-White Archives, which include her photographic prints and negatives, cameras, notes, scrapbooks, correspondence, and original editions of Margaret's works. See the Web site for a complete list of its holdings.

University of Virginia
http://xroads.virginia.edu/~1930s/PRINT/fortune/fortunethumbs.html

This Web site features selected covers of *Fortune* magazine from the 1930s and early 1940s.

World Foto
http://www.worldfoto.org/INDICE.html

This is a great site for anyone interested in seeing photo-essays from around the world.

A Note on Sources

To research this book, I consulted the extensive Margaret Bourke-White Archives at the Special Collections Research Center of Syracuse University Library. Much of my material about Bourke-White's childhood comes from these sources. At Syracuse, I also had the pleasure of listening to a speech Bourke-White gave at the University of Miami in the late 1950s. It was a testament to her fortitude and generosity to hear her lecture at length, with great energy and focus, while suffering from Parkinson's disease.

I also conducted research at New York City's Humanities and Social Sciences Library, Columbia University's Butler Library and Fine Arts Collection, and Barnard College's Lehman Library. Butler Library has original *Life* magazines on its open stacks. These were a pleasure to look through. Reading the original magazines, I was reminded of how much advertising surrounded the iconic photographs of the twentieth century.

Bourke-White's books on World War II, Russia, and India all provided great insight into her social conscience. Bourke-White's *You Have Seen Their Faces* and *Shooting the Russian War* detail the equipment and methods she used in taking her photographs. Her autobiography, *Portrait of Myself*, and Vicki Goldberg's invaluable, consummately researched biography are the sources for many anecdotes in the book.

Exhibition catalogs on Clarence H. White and Margaret Bourke-White were useful sources of information on conceptual issues, in particular *A Collective Vision: Clarence H. White and His Students* by Lucinda Barnes, and *Power and Paper: Margaret Bourke-White: Modernity and the Documentary Mode* by John Stomberg.

The World Wide Web contains hundreds of Bourke-White photos, and quite a few sites devote pages to her. The online encyclopedia Wikipedia was an excellent source for information on the events and movements of the twentieth century. I enjoyed listening to National Public Radio's Web page on Bourke-White, which offers Susan Stamberg's informative interviews with Goldberg and curator Stephen Bennett Phillips, and a brief excerpt of the voice of Margaret Bourke-White telling a snide radio announcer in 1938, "I doubt I'll ever settle down into the normal life of a housewife."

—*Christopher C. L. Anderson*

Index

Advertising photography, 20, 42, 43, 52, 61, 66, 82
Aerial photography, *42*, 58, 75
African Americans, 83, 84, 90
"America" (song), 74–75
American Artists' Congress, 65, 107
American Bar Association, 58
American Youth Congress, 65
Ann Arbor, Michigan, 21
Anti-Semitism, 23
Apartheid, 100, 103
Architectural photography, *26*, 27. *See also* Industrial photography.
Atomic weapons, 89, 105, 108

Battlefield printing presses, 13
Bemis, Alfred Hall "Beme," 31, 35
Bolwell, Charlie, 35
Bound Brook, New Jersey, 8, 9
Bourke-White, Margaret, *6*, *9*, *15*, *21*, *32*, *40*, *69*, 77
- advertising photography, 42, 43, 52, 61, 66, 82
- aerial photography, *42*, 58, 75
- air raid photographs, 72–74, *72*
- American Artists' Congress and, 65, 107
- American Youth Congress and, 65
- architectural photography, *26*, 27
- art and, 17
- autobiography of, 9, 36, 55, 59, 74, 110, 111, 112, 113
- automobile of, 33
- balance of, 40–41
- "Begonia" and, 55–56
- on bombing mission, 78–79
- bomber refueling photographs, 106
- brain surgeries, 113
- at Buchenwald concentration camp, 85–87, 97
- butterfly photographs, 65–66, 67
- Calcutta riot photographs, 97
- as camp counselor, 21
- Carswell Strategic Air Command photographs, *104*, 105–106
- cat of, 111, *111*
- chain gang photograph, 56
- childhood of, 9, *9*, 40–41
- Chrysler Building photographs, 40, *40*
- Cleveland Chamber of Commerce photographs, 30, *30*
- Cleveland public square photograph, 29–30, *30*
- Cleveland Tower building photograph, *26*
- clothing of, 13, *32*, 33, 35, 78

Bourke-White, Margaret *(cont.)*
Communism and, 106–108
in Czechoslovakia, 67–69
death of, 113
divorce of, 25, 27
Dust Bowl photographs, 49–51, 67
Eastern Airlines photographs, 58
education of, 13–14, 15, *15*, 17, 19, 21–23, *21*, 23–24, 25, 31, 43
FBI file on, 107
Fort Peck Dam photographs, *62*, 63
Frank Hague photographs, 64–65
George Patton and, 85
George Washington Bridge photograph, 44
in Germany, 43, 44, 85–91, 97
health of, 10–11, 111–113
as herpetologist, 9, 17, 23, 25, 65
in India, 93, 94, 95, 97–98, 99, 100
in Italy, 82
Joseph Stalin and, 49
journey to North Africa, 76–78
in Korea, 109–110
lecture tour, 74
letter from Amelia Earhart, 44
letters from Jerry Papurt, 85
marriages of, 24, 69–70
Mohandas Gandhi and, 94, 95, *95*, 97–99
mother-in-law of, 24, 25
motion pictures by, 49
name change, 29
Nim Churl-Jin and, 109–110, *110*
nurse photographs, *80*
office of, 41–42
as outer space photojournalist, 106
paper photographs, 66–67, *66*
phrenologist diagnosis of, 14–15
posters of, 78
scarlet fever of, 10–11
as school yearbook editor, 15
separation from Caldwell, 84–85
sharecropper photos, 55
in South Africa, 100–103
in Soviet Union, 44, 47, 48–49, *48*, 71, 73
steel mill photographs, 33–36, *34*, *36*
television play about, 113
Brady, Matthew, 20
Bronx, New York, 8
Brownie cameras, 31
Buchenwald concentration camp, 85, 86

Calcutta, India, 97
Caldwell, Erskine (husband), 52–53, 56, 57–58, 69, *69*
Capa, Robert, 56
Cape Town, South Africa, 101
Carswell Strategic Air Command, *104*, 105–106
Case Western Reserve University, 25
Celluloid, 31
Chapman, Everett "Chappie" (husband), 22, *23*, 24–25
Charka (spinning wheel), 94, 95, *95*
Chrysler Building, 40, *40*, 41–42, *42*
Churl-Jin, Nim, 109–110, *110*
Civil disobedience, 94, 103
Cleveland Chamber of Commerce, 30
Cleveland, Ohio, 25, *26*, 27–28, 29–30, *30*
Cleveland Tower building photo, *26*
Columbia University, 15, 17, 19, 21, 58
Committee on Operations of the Senate, 108
Committee on Public Information (CPI), 12
Communism, 45, 46, 106–108
Communist International (Comintern), 45
Concentration camps, 68, 85, 86–87, *86*
Constitution of the United States, 14, 83
Cooper, Hugh L., *46*
Cornell University, 25
Curtis, Edward S., 20
Czechoslovakia, 67–69

Darien, Connecticut, 111, *111*
Darkrooms, 32
Dear Fatherland, Rest Quietly (Margaret Bourke-White), 86–87, 88–89, 91
Doolittle, Jimmy, 78
Dow, Arthur Wesley, 15, 19
Dust Bowl, 50–51, *50*, 67

Eastern Airlines, 58
Eisenstaedt, Alfred, 113
Engels, Friedrich, 45
Enola Gay (bomber), 89
Evans, Walker, 57
Extermination camps, 68
Eyes on Russia (Margaret Bourke-White), 47

Fascism, 65, 68
Fifteenth Amendment, 83
Flash powder, 35
Flats (Cleveland, Ohio), 27–28
Fort Peck Dam, *62*
Fort Worth, Texas, *104*
Fortune magazine, 8, 37–38, 40, 43, 49–51, 52, 61

G.I. Bill of Rights, 84
Gandhi, Mohandas, 8, 93–94, *95*, 97–99, 103
Germany, 43, 44, 68, 71, 85–91, 97
Graubner, Oscar, *40*, 62–63
Great Britain, 93, 94–95, 96
Great Depression, *50*, 51, 55, 63
Great Plains, 50, *50*

Hague, Frank, 64–65
Halfway to Freedom (Margaret Bourke-White), 100
Hearst news corporation, 107
Herpetology, 9, 17, 23, 25, 65
Hicks, Wilson, 71
Hindus, 97, *98*
Hiroshima, Japan, 89
Hitler, Adolf, 68
Hoover, J. Edgar, 108
House Un-American Activities Committee (HUAC), 107
How the Other Half Lives (Jacob Riis), 64

India, 93–95, *96*, 97–99, *98*, 99–100
  British in, 93, 94–95, 96
  Calcutta, 97
  independence of, 93, 97
  textile industry in, 95
  wealth in, *96*
Indonesia, 96
Industrial photography, 27–28, 33–36, *34*, 39–41, 43, 66, *66*. *See also* Architectural photography.
Ingersoll, Ralph, 70
International Paper Company, 66
Ithaca, New York, 25

Jackson, H. F., 35
Janah, Sunil, 95
Jersey City, New Jersey, 64

de Klerk, F.W., 103
Kodak cameras, 31
Korea, 109–110
Krupp, Afried, 91
Kulas, Elroy, 33–34

Lange, Dorothea, 18–19, 57
Leahy, William D., 89
Leiter, Earl, 33, 36
Lenin, Vladimir, 45
Life magazine, 8, 61–65, *62*, 67, 71, 72, 75, 79, 82, 93, 100–103, 106, 113
Luce, Henry, 37, 61, 62, 107
Lynching, 54

Machine Age, 37, 43, 52
Magnesium flares, 35

Mandela, Nelson, 103
Marx, Karl, 45
McCarthy, Joseph, 108
Moscow, Soviet Union, 71, *72*
Moscowitz, Benjamin, 27
Motion pictures, 49
Muckrakers, 64
Munger family, 21
Muslims, 97, *98*
Mussolini, Benito, 68
"My Country 'Tis of Thee" (song), 74–75

Nagasaki, Japan, 89
New Deal, Montana, 63
New Deal programs, 55
New York, New York, 8–9, 17, 18, 39, *40*, 64
New York Stock Exchange, 37, 51
Nineteenth Amendment, 14
Nocturne: Blue and Gold: Old Battersea Bridge (James Whistler), *18*
Nonviolent protest, 103
North of the Danube (Margaret Bourke-White), 68
Nuclear weapons, 89, 105, 108

Otis Steel mills, 33

Padgitt, Jess, 82
Pakistan, 97
Papurt, Maxwell Jerome "Jerry," 85
Parkinson's disease, 112–113
"Patrick" (automobile), 33
Pegler, Westbrook, 106, 107
Philadelphia *Public Record* newspaper, 57
Philippines, 96
Photography
- aerial, *42*, 58, 75
- architectural, *26*, 27
- Brownie cameras, 31
- celluloid, 31
- darkrooms, 32
- development process, 32, 35
- ethics and, 73–74, 99–100
- flash powder, 35
- Kodak cameras, 31
- lighting, 35
- magnesium flares, 35
- motion pictures, 49
- Pictorialists, 18
- portraits, 20
- "printing black," 63
- remote control, 53
- tripods, 31

Photojournalism, 99–100, 114
Phrenologists, 14–15
Pictorialists, 18
PM magazine, 70
Portrait photography, 20
"Printing black," 63
Proletariat, 45
Purdue University, 24

"Red Scare," 108
Riis, Jacob, 64
Rodchenko, Aleksandr, 43
Roosevelt, Franklin D., 55, 89
Roosevelt, Theodore, 64
Rosenberg, Ethel, 108
Rosenberg, Julius, 108
Russian Revolution, 45

Salt March, 94
Securities and Exchange Commission, 55
Segregation, 83, 90, 100
Shahn, Ben, 57
Sharecropping, 53, 54, *54*, 55–56
Sherwin, John, 33
Shooting the Russian War (Margaret Bourke-White), 21, 73, 74
Sikhs, *98*
Silver City, Nevada, 69
Sita (cat), 111, *111*

Solzhenitsyn, Aleksandr, 49
South Africa, 100–103
apartheid in, 100, 103
mining in, 101–102, *101*
Nelson Mandela and, 103
vineyards in, 102–103
South Korea, 109
Soviet Union, 43, 44, 45, *46*, 71, *72*, 105
American industrialists and, 46, *46*
artists in, 107
collective farms, 48
Communism, 45, 46, 106–107, 108
gulags in, 48–49
industry in, 47, *48*
proletariat, 45
Russian Revolution, 45
"space race," 106
Ukraine, 48
White Nights, 71
"Space race," 106
Stalin, Joseph, 47, 49
Steiner, Ralph, 19
Stomberg, John, 66–67
The Story of Steel booklet, 36

Tenant farming, 53, 54
They Called It "Purple Heart Valley" (Margaret Bourke-White), 82–84
Time magazine, 37, 61
Time-Life Corporation, 107
Tobacco Road (Erskine Caldwell), 52
Tripods, 31
Truman, Harry, 89

Ukraine, 48
Union Trust Bank, 33
University of Michigan, 21–23, *21*, 67

Vassos, John, 42
Vlack, Joe, 22

Watkins, Margaret, 19
Weegee (photojournalist), 56
Whistler, James, 18, *18*
White, Clarence H., 15, 18
White, Joseph (father), 8–9, 11, *11*, 13, 19–20, 21, 23, 36
White, Minnie (mother), 8, 9–10, *11*, 13, 23, 25, 29, 58–59
White, Roger (brother), 9, 11, 23, 25, 58
White, Ruth (sister), 9, 10, 58
Women
first solo flight, 44
flappers, 22
as photojournalists, 114
self-support of, 7
sexual harassment of, 114
in Soviet Union, 47
suffrage movement, 14
in World War II, 75, *80*, 84
World War I and, 22
Women's Air Corps (WAC), 75
Works Progress Administration, 55
World War I, 12, 13, 22
World War II, 71–73, *72*, 82–84
African Americans in, 83, 84
black market, 90–91
bombing missions, 78–79, *79*, 87–88, *88*, 89
concentration camps, 68, 85, 86–87, *86*
Great Depression and, 51
looting, 90–91
Pearl Harbor, 75
women in, 75, *80*, 84
Women's Air Corps (WAC), 75

You Have Seen Their Faces (Erskine Caldwell/Margaret Bourke-White), 52–53, 56–57, 101

About the Author

Christopher C. L. Anderson studied creative writing at Brooklyn College, earning a masters of fine art degree in 2000. His poetry has appeared in *Brooklyn Review*, *Spawn*, and *Crosscurrents*. He has also written for the *Brooklyn Heights Press & Cobble Hill News*. Like Margaret Bourke-White, he loves traveling and learning about different cultures.

Born in Fall River, Massachusetts, he currently lives in the Boreum Hill section of Brooklyn, New York. This is his first book.